Nostradamus and the End of Evils Begun...

Nostradamus and the End of Evils Begun...

by Stewart Robb

Longmeadow Press

Dedicated to my sweet and lovely wife
Marilyn, the soul of the violin.

This 1991 edition is published by
Longmeadow Press
201 High Ridge Road
Stamford, CT 06904

ISBN 0-681-41117-1
Library of Congress Catalog Card TX1-292-460

Printed in the United States of America

0 9 8 7 6 5 4 3 2 1

TABLE OF CONTENTS

Nostradamus

Preface

Hold on to this book. One never can tell what it may foretell. It is my fifth on Nostradamus, most of it in print in 1984, but not in distribution till now. But the cover of the paperback you are holding in your hands dates back 49 years. Orban was a remarkable artist, and his aggressive Arab originally appeared in my own magazine-book, *What The Future Holds*, published in 1942. My third book on the prophet, *The New Nostradamus*, published 47 years ago, contained my following comment on the new Russia and its new leader:

> The Russian river Dnieper has its source near Moscow. Hence it stands for Russia and the government of Russia. So we may interpret: Communism will fail first of all in Russia. A leftist leader will arise who by his propaganda and eloquence will persuade the Muscovites to jettison much of their communistic doctrine for a more easy-going socialism. Possibly a moderate form of democracy will arise in the land of the Dnieper. Who will bring about such a change? Perhaps a successor to Stalin. Perhaps the "ornate" tongued one mentioned earlier in this chapter.

In my same *The New Nostradamus* I tried my luck in interpreting what the prophet had to say about Japan. The Nostra damus prophecy I quoted was taken from Charles Ward's splendid book, *The Oracles of Nostradamus*, first published in the 90's. His translation and identifications read thusly:

> The city of Achem (in the Island of Sumatra) shall be encompassed and assaulted on all sides by a great force of armed men. Their maritime forces (Japan's) shall be weakened by the Occidentals.
> Upon this kingdom (Japan) a great destruction shall come, and such as enter in shall come under the vengeance of the wrath of God.

My comment followed:

There can be no question that this prediction means that a nation attacking the Dutch East Indies (and specifically Sumatra) will be defeated by the Americans. The word "Occidentals" means those who inhabit land over the sea, west of France. This is further borne out by another unmistakable reference to America in the quatrain in which Nostradamus referred to the Occident breaking away from England.

Of course, in 1944 I knew nothing about atom bombs or their effect, so my comment was puzzled:

Japan's doom is foreshadowed in a curious way that points to something even worse than Allied air blitz of Tokyo and Japan's other big cities. It is evident that Japan's navy will be crushed and that air bombardment of Japan itself is now occurring on a large scale, but Allied occupation of Japan proper is *not indicated*.

In fact, a great catastrophe, — probably an earthquake and tidal wave — is forecast by Nostradamus.

Not quite! And yet, more than quite.

So, I say again, save the book in your hands. It may hold surprises in years to come.

Nota Bene

The book in your hands is different from any other books on Nostradamus, including my own.

The thesis herein is that prophecies of disaster and doom that have not yet occurred need never occur. Any predicted evil can be de-clawed, circumvented or prevented.

Take unfulfilled predictions of doom — no matter how truly prophetic their source — *at best*, as warnings of evils to be nullified by the ever-present power of prayer.

Fear no evil—even nuclear. Says Mrs.Eddy:"The material atom is an outlined falsity of consciousness, which can gather additional evidence of consciousness and life only as it adds lie to lie. Atomic action is Mind, not matter." That Mind — with a capital M — is not the inherently powerless human mind, but the Mind of the Lord. So fear neither instant atomization nor agonizing torture and death from an earth-wrapping fallout. Said Isaiah: "He will destroy in this mountain the face of the covering cast over all people, and the veil that is spread over all nations." "He will swallow up death in victory; and the Lord God will wipe away tears off all faces; and the rebuke of His people shall He take away from off all the earth; for the Lord hath spoken it."

"As birds flying, so will the Lord of hosts defend Jerusalem."

—Isaiah

Who Was Nostradamus?

Michel de Nostredame was an involuntary prophet, though he wisely cultivated his God-given faculty by prayer and meditation. He was born December 14, 1503, in St. Remy, Provence, France. His father was a very busy and successful notary public. Both parents were of gentle birth. It is said that a knowledge of mathematics and the faculty of prophecy both descended to the son from his mother's family. It is also said he was of Jewish birth. Nostradamus states that he was of the prophetically-gifted Lost Tribe of Issachar.

Nostradamus won extraordinary fame and repute as a doctor, curing thousands in the plague years by unorthodox remedies — mainly by one made from roses! Unhappily, however, his skill was not enough to save his young wife and two children from the pestilence. Broken hearted, he took to the road — probably for distraction — and traveled through France and Italy.

After his return from his travels, Nostradamus settled in Salon, France, and here it was that he began to prophesy, first modestly publishing almanacs. These were a success. In March, 1555, appeared his first book of prophecies, consisting of a preface to his infant son Cesar, followed by three hundred and fifty-four "quatrains," or four-line verse predictions. This book was called *The True Centuries (Les vrayes Centuries)* — a "Century" being not a hundred years but a collection of one hundred stanzas. His notoriety grew. He was summoned to the court of Henry II and his his wife, Catherine de Medici, and there he was wonderfully well entertained.

The fame of Nostradamus became firmly established and

his latter years appear to have been happy. His neighbors held him in awe and respect; King, princes and prelates beat a path to his door; he was never in want. Chavigny writes, "Those who came to France sought Nostradamus as the only thing to be seen there." He published more of his verse prophecies, dedicating them to Henry II of France. When Charles IX came to the throne, Nostradamus' star rose still higher. King Charles recognized the sage for what he was: hero of the plague years and one of the most brilliant graduates of Avignon and Montpellier, the most famous school of medicine in France. So he made this great scholar his Royal Physician.

Such was the career of Nostradamus. He died in 1566, a prophet with honor in his own country.

Suggestions On Interpreting Nostradamus

If the reader understands French, he should read the quatrains in French and not first in the English version. The "authorities" and sciolists on Nostradamus sometimes inject words and ideas into the translation that are not in the original text.

Even if the reader knows next to nothing of French, he should still make an attempt to check the translation against the original, whenever that original is given. Even with only a smattering of remembered school French, he may sometimes discover that the English version is farther afield from the original than need be. He may also discover that the more literally precise the translation, the more powerful the prophecy.

Nostradamus not only wrote in French but was a Frenchman to the core. Prophets of all lands are patriots, intensely interested in the destiny of their own people and rulers. So when Nostradamus mentions "the government," "the king," "the great people," etc., he is referring to *his own* government, *his own* king, and *his own* people. When he intends the government of America, or the king of England, Germany or Poland, he is quite capable of saying so, and does.

He devotes the greater part of his prophetic attention to history's most momentous periods. Hence the many quatrains on the French Revolution, the Napoleonic era — and the coming Arab antichrist. But in all this he is looking outwards from *France*.

To illustrate by parallel: Suppose an American Nostradamus writing, say, in the eighteenth century, were to make predictions concerning "the president," or, "the Government." The safest and most intelligent interpretation would be to assume the president or the government of America was meant, not, for instance, the president or government of Brazil. But this little piece of common-sense advice is what too many interpreters of Nostradamus have never heard, and jokers are wild.

The interpreter of the prophet should not be too imaginative. If he finds the word "inundation" in the text, it is not too likely that the meaning is "invasion." There are a few exceptions to this safe rule.

If he lights on an anagram, that is, a word with its letters transposed, as for instance *Rapis* for *Paris, or noir* for *roi,* he should be aware that these occur in *Les Vrayes Centuries* simply because the prophet-poet was a child of his age. He was not attempting to conceal or muddy his meaning. Ronsard and other contemporaries of the seer also used anagrams — and they were not even attempting to write cloudy prophecy. Anagrams were the order of the day.

Synecdoche was also in order for Nostradamus. He uses it, though fairly rarely. He may name a river for the area or land through which the river runs.

In interpreting the quatrains, a knowledge of history will be greatly helpful, particularly against the error of Nostradamians who interpret as future a prophecy already magnificently fulfilled. He will not make the error, for instance, of thinking that Nostradamus predicted the three Kennedy brothers, when the three brothers predicted were the three kings of France: Louis XVI, Louis XVIII, and Charles X.

Here, now, are some actual examples of fulfilled prophecies of the French seer which are currently mistaken for the shape of things to come. Clear your mind, reader, and read them aright:

> The great Cornerstone will die three leagues from the Rhone;
> Flee, two close kinsmen, flee destructive monster:
> For Mars will make the most horrible throne
> Of the Cock and the Eagle, and of the three brothers of France
>
> (VIII,46)

One's knowledge of French history makes it possible or easy to determine whether this prophecy has been fulfilled. Seek first a clue, and work outward from it. For instance, one may take as a starting point the last four words of line three, *most horrible throne.* When did France have her most horrible throne? During the terror!

You will quickly see that the three brothers are not the Kennedy brothers(!!!) but Louis XVI, the pacifist king who was guillotined, and his two brothers who fled the Terror and after the downfall of Napoleon returned to rule their land as Louis XVIII and Charles X respectively.

Be careful! The best of Nostradamians, as well as the poorest, have muddied and mutilated the master. So, let's take some quatrains that have been interpreted amiss and attempt to set the record straight so that he who runs astray may read aright:

One prophecy has been interpreted as predicting the utter doom of the British Isles, which are to sink under the ocean! The quatrain read:

La Grande Bretaigne comprinse d'Angleterre,
Viendra par eaux si haut a inonder
La Ligue neuve d'Ausonne fera guerre
Que contre eux ils se viendront bander.

(III,70)

Great Britain, comprising England
Will be very highly inundated by the waters.
The new League of Ausona will make war
But just against those who band against it.

Nostradamus appears to have been the first man in the world to pen the words Great Britain — *with England comprised.* England became Great Britain thirty-seven years after the death of the prophet. James the Sixth of Scotland ascended the English throne as James the First, and a year later, on October 24, 1604, he assumed the title "King of Great Britain."

The floods described in the quatrain commenced in January, 1607. They did not submerge the Isles, but they did batter down the Somersetshire dykes, and, as Ward says, "overflowed the country for thirty miles in length and six miles inland, to the destruction of all property and most of the inhabitants." This was an event important enough for the prophet's pen.

The forming of the new league of Ausona took place at a time between the two predicted events. Ausona is a poetic name for Rome or Italy used by Vergil, Ovid and other Latin writers.

This Italian League was indeed new, as Nostradamus says, for it was a renewal of the defensive Holy League (1526) between the King of France. the Pope, and the Venetians.

Now note the utter closeness of the dates of the events predicted:

1603, England becomes literally Great Britain.
1604, The title of King of Great Britain is assumed by the king.
1606, The new Italian defensive League is formed.
1607, The floods come.

So the prophecy was fulfilled, and without England sinking into the ocean.

Another quatrain sometimes dusted off by Nostradamians and incorrectly applied to the future reads thus:

Classe Gauloise n'approches de Corseigne,
Moins de Sardaigne, tu t'en répentiras:
Trestous mourrez frustrés de L'aide grogne:
Sang nagera: captif ne me croiras.

(III,87)

French fleet, do not approach Corsica,
Even less Sardinia, you will repent of it:
All will die, frustrated of aid from the pig:
Blood will swim: captive, you won't believe me!

Fulfilled to the letter in 1655. A French squadron, commanded by the Chevalier de la Ferriére met its doom precisely in the area described. Le Pelletier states that the entire fleet was lost, and that no aid came from Cape Pourceau. Did some princes of noble blood lose their lives? Well, at least one did, maybe more. As for mention of the "captive" who won't believe the prophet, master pilot Jean de Rian, nicknamed Le Captif, had been a galley slave.

Another prophecy, misinterpreted by fundamentalists and others as weirdly occult, is not so:

With rod in hand put in the middle of Branches,
He moistens both the limb and the foot in the wave:
A fear and voice shaking through the sleeves:
Splendor divine, the divine is seated nearby.

This is one of two quatrains introducing the prophecies and Nostradamus to the reader. The prophet is ready to capture the divine inspiration on paper. He picks up the pen (the rod), grasps it with his five fingers (the Branches) then dips the pen into the inkwell, creating a tiny wave. He is now ready for the divine afflatus.

Challenge To Skeptics

William Lyon Phelps wrote of Nostradamus: "It is not surprising that as the old fellow said so much he occasionally said something that might be applied to historical or contemporary persons in the public eye. Curiously enough, only last night I was reading in the eighteenth of the hitherto unpublished journals of Boswell; in the year 1792, when hell broke loose in France, he was making a peaceful journey down in Cornwall and on September 14, dined copiously and elegantly at Lord Camelford's; and, writes Boswell,

> We talked naturally a great deal of the horrid scenes in France. Lord Camelford mentioned the Prophecies of Nostradamus, called his *Centenaires*, some of which had been pointedly fulfilled in the very years foretold. This his Lordship *admitted*, but maintained that it was only chance, because the greatest part had not happened; and proved that if you would throw upon paper a number of events as predictions, no matter what, some of them would be fulfilled. This I did not like, supposing the predictions to be very *circumstantial*, so as to multiply very much the *chances* against hitting a *future fact*. I must see this curious Collection of *second sight* and examine what has happened or been proved to correspond.

Suppose Names Are Predicted, Even Two At A Time!

Boswell answered shrewdly. What proves or disproves a man a prophet is not merely the number of his "fulfilled" predictions, but their *quality*. For instance, suppose an American prophet who had written reams of seeming jargon suddenly came out plump with the following prediction, and a hundred years before the event: "Lincoln in a theater, Booth is the assas-

18

sin."

It would be foolish to question such seership: he would be established as an authentic prophet. Such a prophecy would be so beyond the stab of chance that no matter what else he had written, this one line alone would make him a portentous figure, awing even the puzzled skeptic.

What No Skeptic Can Explain

What shall we say then of Nostradamus, who wrote many prophecies as wonderful as the hypothetical American prediction. Take for instance the following: "One betrayer will be titled Narbon, and Saulce..."

This is not a whit less wonderful than would be the "Lincoln-Booth" prediction. The only difference is that the names and history are French instead of American; the names named are those of a French minister of war and a grocer instead of an American president and an actor. Now a skeptic who is an American would admit the wonderfulness of the "Lincoln-Booth" prophecy *because he knows the history.* So he must admit the wonderfulness of the French prophecy when he learns the story behind it. The history related in the French prophecy is as true, and of more earth-shaking importance than the assassination of Lincoln.

Lighting Cannot Strike Forty Times In One Place

George Bernard Shaw once said, "Great art is either easy or impossible." The same is true of prophecy. If you can prophesy at all you should be able to repeat the performance, because you possess a power. This was true of Nostradamus. He turned out prophecies as Bach turned out fugues. He named more than a dozen historical figures of importance who had not even been born when he wrote; he named them in at least three instances *two at a time,* and — if it increases the wonder — characterized them as well. Besides, in my book, *Nostradamus on Napoleon, Hitler and the present Crisis* there are quoted and interpreted over forty quatrains which apply accurately to the Corsican-born French Emperor. If Nostradamus were stabbing in the dark, there might conceivably be found prophecies of his applicable to a variety of historical personages, but there would not

19

be as many as *forty on the one man*. Lightning cannot strike
so many times in one place.

Another Prophecy Beyond The Stab Of Chance

"Suppose the predictions to be very circumstantial," said
Boswell, "so as to multiply very much the chances against
hitting a *future fact*." No need to suppose. They *are*. Dr. Phelps
opined that it was not surprising the old fellow should occasionally "say something that might be applied to historical or contemporary persons in the public eye." So let us see how likely
it was for Nostradamus to off even *one* of these "somethings":

The year 1727 in October,
The king of Persia taken by those of Egypt:
...great opprobrium to the cross.

Out of curiosity I took this quatrain to a professor of
mathematics at Columbia University, requesting him to calculate the odds against its fulfillment being merely a lucky hit.
Here are his calculations:

As the prophecies cover the years between 1555 and 3797,
Nostradamus had — if no judgment were involved —

1) One chance in 2242 (i.e., 3797 minus 1555) of guessing
   the right year.
2) One chance in 12 of guessing the right month.
3) One chance in $n(n-1)/2$ of guessing the right nations, n
   standing for the number of nations in existence at the
   time the prophecy is due to be fulfilled. If there were 15
   nations in existence at this time — actually there were
   many more — there would be 105 ways of selecting two
   of them.
4) One chance in two of picking the victor.
5) One chance in two of correctly stating the effect on the
   cross of the outcome of the war. In this case, it is "great
   opprobrium."

Now let us see. The total possible chance of a random stroke
is one in: 2242 x 12 x 105 x 2 x 2 — or — 11,299,680.
Actually, for obvious reasons, the odds are incalculably

greater.

"1792, When Hell Broke Loose In France"

Next I showed the mathematics professor the following passage from Nostradamus' Dedicatory Epistle to Henry the Second:

> . . . then will come the beginning including in itself what will long endure, and starting that same year there will be the greatest persecution of the Christian Church, worse than that which took place in Africa, and this will culminate in the year 1792 which people will think to be a renovation of time...

A new era is a renovation of time, and France's new era — one of the most important and fateful in all history — was the royalty-uprooting Revolution. Now 1792, the date given by Nostradamus, brings us right into the thick of the Revolution. The prophet associates this year and this new era with a terrible persecution of the Christian Church. When Nostradamus wrote, the Church was securely established in France. The country was Catholic, it still is. Yet 1792 brings us into the midst of a frightful persecution of the clergy, with few precedents in world history, and with none in France. So much did the Reds of the Revolution hate Christianity that they abolished the "Anno Domini" calendar, and proclaimed Year One of the Republic. When? Specifically, on September 21, 1792, not a year earlier, not a year later. Even the months were changed, and Carlyle writes with scornful humor:

> Autumnal Equinox, at midnight for the meridian of Paris, in the year whilom Christian 1792, from that moment shall the New Era reckon itself to begin. *Vendemiaire, Brumaire, Frimaire;* or as one might say, in mixed English, *Vintagearious, Fogarious, Frostarious:* these are our three Autumn months. *Nivose, Pluviose, Ventose,* or say, *Snowous, Rainous, Windous,* Make our Winter season. *Germinal, Floreal, Prairial,* or *Buddal, Floweral, Meadowal,* are our Spring season. *Messidor, Thermidor, Fructidor,* that is to say (*dor* being Greek for *gift*) *Reapidor, Heatidor, Fruitidor* are Republican Summer. These twelve, in a singular manner, divide the Republican Year. Then as to minuter subdivisions, let us venture at once on a bold stroke: adopt your decimal subdivision... There are three dec-

ades, then, in each of the months; which is very regular; and the *Decadi*, or Tenthday, shall always be the "Day of Rest." And the Christian Sabbath, in that case? Shall shift for itself!

"They will *think* it to be a renovation of time," writes the prophet. Surely! Did not this anti-Christian new era foolishness officially end on January 1, 1806, and the French return to the Christian calendar, which they still use?

The Odds Mount Up!

Nostradamus has associated these facts exactly as the historians have done. When they write of the persecution of the Church, they discuss at the same time Year One of the Republic, mentioning that this new era began in 1792, and that it was a direct result of the anti-Christian program of the Republicans.

"What are the odds here?" I asked Professor Siceloff.

"2242, since the month is not given, but just the year."

"But," I said, "Nostradamus has correctly associated *two* historical facts with this year, not one. That must increase the odds greatly."

"Actually the odds are incalculable," he replied.

But keeping these odds on a conservative and calculable basis (absurdly low), the chances of the prophet accidentally hitting off both these dated predictions is one in 11,299,680 X 2242 - or — 25,311,283,200.

And these are not the only prophecies to which Nostradamus has affixed the correct dates! There are at least three more.

Did Nostradamus Stumble Upon Franco?

As to the undated prophecies, their analysis must be qualitative rather than quantitative; yet an approximation to a quantitative analysis may be made of even some of these. Take for instance the quatrain:

The assembly will go out from the castle of Franco,
The ambassador not satisfied will make a schism:
Those of the Riviera will be involved,
And they will deny the entry to the great gulf.

(9.16)

De castel Franco sortira l'assemblee,
L'ambassadeur non plaissant fera scisme:
Ceux de Riviere seront en la meslee
Et au grand goulphre desnieront l'entree.

In February, 1941, the Spanish Generalissimo met Mussolini on the Riviera and refused to allow the axis troops to pass through Spain to get to Gibraltar. Observe that this quatrain is about a meeting, that it names Franco, mentions the Riviera and states the conclusion correctly.

Despite the fact that Nostradamus sometimes uses place-names for persons (such playing on names is not unusual in the poetry of sixteenth century France) and despite the fact that the normal way of writing *castel Franco* is *Castelfranco,* let us start from skeptical scratch with an admission that all we know about *castel Franco* is that the name Franco occurs in it. Even so, the odds against this prediction being a stab in the dark are very high. Together with the name Franco, which occurs only once in the writings of the prophet, there is mentioned the Riviera and the denial of entry to the great gulf. To a Frenchman the great gulf is the Mediterranean and its entry is most certainly at Gibraltar.

If mention of the Riviera is but a happy hit, it is none the less extraordinary. The map of Europe is dotted with thousands of place-names. The odds against the prophet naming the Riviera together with Franco are equal in number to the number of European place names it is possible to mention. Working on a basis of chance, one name would be likely to be as significant as another. Yet the Riviera is the very name that is significant *above all others.* However, for the sake of the fearful skeptic, let us reduce the odds to a *thousand* — though obviously they are *much greater.*

The last line of the quatrain may be treated in the same manner. The conclusion of the meeting is correctly and precisely stated: "They will deny the entry to the great gulf." Ask the question, "In *how* many ways may a meeting conclude?" Thousands — putting it mildly! Yet for the skeptic's sake, we again reduce the odds to a *thousand.*

Result: one chance in a million (1000 x 1000) that the naming of Franco is merely a happy hit. Actually, the odds against its being so defy calculation.

Total Odds For Three Prophecies Only

However, in each case accepting the calculated odds, the probability that *all three prophecies* treated so far by the law of averages are lucky hits, is:

$$\frac{1}{11{,}299{,}680} \times \frac{2}{2240} \times \frac{3}{1{,}000{,}000}$$

Or, one chance in 25,311,283,200,000,000!

Mind you, this is a modest figure. Suppose I were to start work on the forty odd prophecies referable only to Napoleon, or the sixty odd on the French Revolution — or both together. You can understand that the number would mount up!

Interpreting Nostradamus Before The Event

My Scribner book on Nostradamus contained the asseveration that it was practically impossible to interpret the quatrains correctly until history had caught up with them. Subsequently I learned that one could do considerably better than that. Frequently, when part of a prophecy *begins* to come to pass it becomes possible to interpret the rest, because one has a clue to work with. During World War Two my own batting average of correct interpretation before the event turned out to be very high. Indeed, much better than I expected. The quatrains concerned were unusually specific. My one error was giving the date of Hitler's fall as 1943 — and this was from an interpretation of the St. Odile prophecy, not of Nostradamus. But even here it is possible this may not have been more than six months out. (Nostradamus, by the way, did not date the war's end.)

Here, in brief, are the interpretations made and publicized *before the event:*

1. That Hitler could never get Gibraltar, and that Franco would deny access to the rock at a meeting on the Riviera.
2. That a Japanese attack on Sumatra would be followed by the first Japanese naval reverses. (News release issued by Scribner's, December, 1941).
3. That Hitler would build a bridge over the Danube, and that this action would in some way be associated with his "vexing of Italy."
4. That Stalingrad would certainly hold, and that the battle for the city would mark the successful turning point of the war for the Russians. (This prediction was given by me on John B. Kennedy's radio program and published

in the N.Y. World-Telegram and other papers during Stalingrad's darkest hour).

5. That the Allies would attack through Italy. (Stated at Town Hall Lecture, Armistice night, 1942).
6. That "The Italian power will be utterly laid low for following the footsteps of its great neighbor."
7. That Mussolini was "to fall through trouble at home of a revolutionary nature."
8. That the Royal Air Force would grow stronger and stronger and that their air-raids over Germany would practically bring about the collapse of Naziland.
9. That the question of Anglo-American Union would come up after the war. It did — and will again.

Except for the too-early timing of Hitler's doom, not one solitary statement may be found in any of my writings on the seer that has been falsified by events.

Let us look at some of these prophecies that found their fulfillment during the course of the Hitler War. One of the most remarkable is quatrain 16 of Century Nine. I quote again:

The assembly will go out from the castle of Franco,
The ambassador not satisfied will make a schism:
Those of the Riviera will be involved,
And they will deny the entry to the great gulf.

Correctly reading this extremely lucid prophecy, I was able to forecast that the Caudillo would meet the Axis powers on the Riviera, that there would be a big pow-wow, and that Hitler and Mussolini would fail to get Gibraltar. Every single day for several months before the event I carefully scanned the front pages of the newspapers, in the expectation that such a meeting would take place. It did. On February 13, 1941 the New York Times featured the meeting in a lengthy article and headlined *Riviera*. Most of our news commentators believed the Axis parley would result in Axis success, but I confidently awaited a contrary outcome, and was justified. Commenting on this quatrain in my Scribner book, which was published in October of 1941, I wrote,

After the war, history books summarizing the part played

by Spain in the present conflict will mention that Franco met Mussolini on the Riviera, and refused to cooperate with the Axis to let troops pass through Spain to Gibraltar.[1]

Even this was going very much out on a limb, for did not the world believe at that time that Hitler was strong enough to falsify such a prophecy at any moment? On radio programs at that time, I confidently stated, "The ranter will never get the rock!"

Note, too, how the Franco prophecy points in the direction of an Allied victory, for if Hitler had won the war he would thereby obtain Gibraltar and anything else he craved.

The defeat of Hitler's Nipponese partner is foretold in the following prose prophecy of Nostradamus, sent out at my request as a news release by Scribner's, in December, 1941:

"The city of Achem (in the Island of Sumatra) will be encompassed and assaulted on all sides by a great force of armed men. Their maritime forces (Japan's) will be weakened by the Occidentals.

Upon this kingdom (Japan) a great desolation will come, and the great cities will be depopulated, and such as enter in will come under the vengeance of the wrath of God.
(from Ward's interpretation in *Oracles of Nostradamus*)

There is no double talk here. The prophecy means that a nation attacking the Dutch East Indies (and specifically Sumatra) will be defeated by those of the Western World. *Achem* was interpreted as Sumatra over ninety years ago by Nostradamian Charles Ward, and no other dictionary definition exists. *Occidentals* means those who inhabit the land over the sea, west of France. This is borne out by another prediction of Nostradamus, in which he writes of the American Revolution:

The Occident will be free of the British Isles,
Not satisfied, sad rebellion...

This News Release aroused a great deal of interest and speculation and became helpful and truthful wartime propaganda. On January 3, 1942, it was quoted in a review of my book by the Chicago Sun, Mr. Tracy York writing skeptically, "At least we have Nostradamus out on a limb now with a prophecy that must fall within our time..." On January 27, the prophecy appeared in Benjamin De Casseres' column, with a favorable comment. The same month the Netherlands purchasing Commission made several thousand photostat copies of the Release, and some of these were sent to the West Coast. On February 12 a business letter was addressed from the West Coast to the Commission, which read in part:

> Nothing can be certain in times like these, and the situation at Singapore is certainly indicative of what I mean. I am sincerely hopeful that the predictions of Nostradamus will prove correct, and that the Japanese will face their first and important reversal in the attempt to invade Sumatra.

Two days later the prophecy came to life: on February 14, Japan *began* the battle for the Dutch East Indies with an attack on Sumatra. Up to this time she had had smashing successes. Now she was to suffer scarcely less smashing naval defeats. Twenty-two Japanese ships were lost. And since then other naval disasters (e.g., Midway and Coral Sea), weakened our enemy's maritime forces. Note that the gentleman writing the Purchasing Commission interpreted the prophecy more correctly than did the Chicago Sun critic. Nostradamus did not predict *immediate* defeat for the Japanese with the attack on Sumatra. Their maritime forces were not then to be destroyed, but "weakened." After that came the destruction of their cities, above all of Hiroshima, "under the wrath of God." — though I think this was a vile deed on our part.

Rolfe Boswell, author of *Nostradamus Speaks,* went even farther out on a limb than I did, predicting our very entry into the war via the Japanese route. Certainly if our government at Washington had been able to take heed of Nostradamus in time, we would have been better prepared for Pearl Harbor. The ancient Hebrews heeded prophecy.

Should we not do likewise?

The Foes Of Democracy
Object To Nostradamus

His lines are no less trenchant today. Measure their might by what their effect has been on the foes of democracy. I received a little inkling of this shortly after the appearance of *Nostradamus on Napoleon and Hitler*.

One sign of opposition was a letter to *Scribner's* from the rabidly isolationist *Occult Digest* (Chicago), received two days before Pearl Harbor:

> My dear friends:
> We are returning under separate cover the review copy of Robb's Nostradamus. It has long been known, and widely commented upon, that nowhere in the Nostradamus predictions did he even mention America. Now, to arbitrarily make his predictions indicate that we are to have "Union Now" with Britain, is nothing more than propaganda, and cheaply done, of which we will have no part. Incidentally, the writer is English and French, and not "pro- German" — but definitely so pro-American that such propaganda is unwelcome in our columns. Sorry.
> Sincerely,
> Miss Marie Harlowe

Apparently this universally-known "fact" that nowhere did Nostradamus mention America, must have been furnished from some occult source, for its truth was not to be found on earth.

About the same time I received a specially-printed postal card. Its author signed himself *Paul Sapart, eau de Cologne specialist* (Winchell suggested this be changed to "woe de Cologne"). Part of his message ran, "Democracy, Liberty, Baloney!" while underneath these uplifting words could be read:

Nostradamus: an astronomer and a prophet. As an astronomer he never knew his "eyes" from a hole in the ground. As a prophet (like all prophets) he was a sophist whose lucubrations can be interpreted for the service of any cause. He would have made a good fisherman. P.S.

Since then I heard that Mr. Sapart had a change of heart dating from Pearl Harbor, after which he sent out printed postal cards playfully calling the Emperor of Japan "a son of the beach." So all was forgiven and perhaps the publicity brought him some custom!

---

[1] In my 1940 lectures I stated there would be a meeting on the Riviera, wherein Franco would deny Gibraltar.

Nostradamus As Propaganda

The best instance of the power of prophecy as propaganda is Nostradamus. His verses are a might weapon for good or ill, just as is the Bible. They are essentially the propaganda of truth, because he was a true seer, though fallible. He foretells the rise and fall of rulers, empires, organizations, parties, cliques. His words can boost morale. They can produce leaden thoughts of defeat.

Les Vrayes Centuries has been labeled propaganda from the moment it first appeared in 1555. Though launched without in interpretative comment it was attacked almost immediately, and so was he. Videl, Couillard and others wrote bitter books on his "seditions" and "falsities." On one occasion the Parisian populace burned him in effigy. Fortunately the famed physician and seer won the favor and protection of a far-sighted royalty.

The next century saw the forging of "Nostradamus" prophecies for use as propaganda against Cardinal Mazarin. The skillful fraud was not discovered for two centuries.

In 1781 the writings of the prophet were placed on the Catholic Index of Forbidden Books In the 19th century the Imperial authorities under Napoleon Third confiscated the quatrains as interpreted by the learned Abbé Torné Chavigny. One of the objectionable verses read:

By the fall of two bastard things
Nephew by blood will occupy the empire;
There will be battle in Lectoyre,
Nephew will fold his flag for fear.

(8.43)

Napoleon Third, who was precisely a "nephew by blood" occupied the empire after the fall of two bastard governments

(Louis Philippe's and the republic). *Lectoyre* is a perfect anagram of *Le Torcy,* which a French Atlas says, "lies on the imperial route from Mezieres to Sedan." The battle of Sedan marked the Nephew's end as Emperor. No wonder he exclaimed after reading one of the seized volumes, "This terrifies and enervates the imagination!"

And so we see that through the troubled centuries the verses of Europe's greatest prophet have proved potent as propaganda. With good reason: they are truthful, inspirational, and frequently "on the nose."

"You had better watch out for yourself," Mrs. Brong said to me one day over the phone, congratulating me on a broadcast. I had just given the St. Odile Prophecy over station WNEW. The response was gratifying. Seventy-three letters which poured into the station asked where copies of the *The Doom of Germany* might be procured. So I took my manuscript to King's on 6th avenue and had more than 500 copies printed. They went like hotcakes. But I made enemies, as well as friends.

One day a man barged into the printing office. "Did you print this pamphlet?" he asked Mr. King angrily, holding up a copy of *The Doom of Germany.* "Yes," said Mr. King. "Then where is the author?" "I don't know," said the printer, who did know, but had begun to smell liquor. Later he told me, "When I refused to give him your address he began to threaten, so I had to make him get out."

In a letter addressed to "Booktab Stewart Robb" an anonymous "son of Nostradamus" jeered, "You feel pretty safe in America, don't you!"

Yes, I did. Totally.

"I didn't realize it when I signed you up," worried Godfrey Bergman said to me in November, 1942, "but I don't think we had better go on with this. My mother lives in Holland." Bergman was my lecture manager, and had hired Town Hall for me for Armistice night. However, his partners, Messers Troob and Blumenthal succeeded in persuading him to go through with it. So on the evening of the day on which we commemorate victory over Germany I was able to unfold to a very receptive audience the reassuring words that we would invade the Boot, that the Italian power would be utterly laid low for following the footsteps of its great neighbor, and that

Hitler would be carried in an iron cage by his own revolted army men before a successful allied invasion of Naziland. Was this coincidence, or destiny? And was the iron cage a submarine headed Argentina-ward? (Spruille Braden thought so.)

Attention of all our pro-Nazis was called to interpretations of the seer when Arthur Hale broadcast this item on *Confidentially Yours:*

> We told you the other night about a prophecy interpreted by the Nostradamus authority, Stewart Robb. Now we learn that the Nazis have their own official book on Nostradamus. As expected, it contains none of the prophecies which American experts interpret as forecasting Hitler's doom.
>
> What's more we find that there is an English version of the Nazi book, published by a firm in Sweden. Why has it been translated? Possibly to convince Britishers and Americans that Hitler victory is inevitable.

Inventions Foreseen By Nostradamus And Other Prophets

Nostradamus has five prophecies on the submarine. Four remain unfulfilled. The fulfilled prophecy concerns Hitler's failure to prevent our supplies from reaching the British Isles. The "eye of the sea" is the periscope:

> From where he thought to cause famine to come,
> From there will come abundance of supplies,
> The eye of the sea watches like a greedy dog,
> While one nation gives the other oil, wheat.

(4.15)

The following quatrain describes a tank-submarine not yet invented. When it is set on the shore the enemy can speed to the walls of Paris:

> When the terrestrial and aquatic fish
> Is set on the shore by the strong wave,
> Its form strange, pleasing, and yet terrible,
> Then the enemy will come from the sea and soon reach the walls.

(1.29)

Its appearance is "strange," which it would be to the vision of the 16th century Frenchman, and probably would to us; it is "pleasing" because streamlined; it is "terrible" because it can treacherously approach under water to appear unexpectedly for a blitzkrieg.

Quatrain 13 of Century Three describes a fleet of ships:

> By lightning on the arch, gold and silver melted,
> Of the two captives the one will eat the other
> Of the most widely extended city,
> When the fleet can swim under water.

No part of the quatrain is clear today except the last line.

In quatrain 5 of Century Two the fish described is obviously a form of submarine, since it is used for making war, and a fleet commander comes out of it:

When there is iron and a letter enclosed in a fish,
He who will then make war will go out from it,
He will have his fleet well rowed through the sea,
Appearing near the Latin land.

Elsewhere the far-sighted Frenchman makes reference to both submarine and airplane:

The scourges past, the world diminished,
For a long time peace, the lands inhabited.
People will travel safely through the sky, land, sea and wave,
Then wars will break out anew.

(1.63)

Note how casual, almost blasé, is the reference to travel by air. Nostradamus seems not to wonder at men flying. Such sights were so common in his prophetic visions that he expresses no more surprise at them than we do. This is typical of the Frenchman, whose prophecies seldom express a feeling of wonder.

Much meaning is packed into that expression, "sea and wave." Ships travel through the waves: submarines through the *sea*

In a prophecy referable to Mussolini or some later leader of Italy, the seer says:

The armaments will fight in the sky a long time,
The tree fallen in the midst of the city,
Vermin, mange, sword, firebrand in his face,
Then the monarch of Italy will succumb.

The first line of the French text reads, *Les armes battre au ciel longue saison. Armes* is more literally translated as "armaments" than "armies."

Two other quatrains which foretell air warfare have been interpreted elsewhere in this book:

The year 1999 seventh month,
A great king of terror will descend from the skies . . .

The Oriental will leave his seat . . .
He will pierce through the sky . . .

But one of the most amazing prophecies of the French seer
is one in which he actually names the inventor of the balloon:
Joseph Michael Montgolfier, French scientist, is celebrated for
his invention of the hot-air balloon, which was named after
him. One of the earliest uses of his airship was military. A
man in the look-out basket was near the hole:

There will go from Mont Gaulfier and Aventine
One who from the hole will warn the army.
The booty will be taken between two rocks,
The renown of Sextus Cornerstone will fail.

(5.57)

The power of this prophecy may easily be proved by expe-
riment. Show the quatrain to someone who has never heard of
Montgolfier and he will be unable to make head or tail of the
second line. But explain the name and the line will be clear to
him.

The prophecy is beyond the batting average of chance. If
Mont-Gaulfier is not a prediction of the Montgolfier balloon
the likelihood of anything else in the stanza bearing any possible relation to the celebrated name or the period will be very
remote. Mont Gaulfier and Montgolfier are the same name. In
French au is pronounced *o*; and encyclopedias list the name
only once.

Mention of Sextus Cornerstone, or the Pope, adds weight
to the interpretation that Nostradamus was alert to the meaning of his visions. Pius the Sixth was kidnaped by Napoleon's
men and died a prisoner in France.

The French seer may have also predicted the use of coal gas:

White coal will be driven from black,
Made prisoner . . .

(4.85)

He seems to have known in advance about the telescope,
and that the scientific advancement it would further would in
turn create in the minds of many a less devout attitude to God:

36

Heavenly bodies without end will be visible to the eye,
Obscuration will come for these reasons
Body, forehead comprehended, sense, head and invisible,
Diminishing the sacred prayers.

(4.25)

Le Pelletier interprets:
When the perfection of optical instruments will have permitted
one to distinguish stars beyond the range of the eye, which one
will assume to be worlds, gravitating endlessly in the depths of
the sky, one will draw from this discovery rationalizations hostile
to religious beliefs. The materialists, subordinating the soul to
the body and recognizing neither God nor superior spirits, will
deliver a blow to traditional worship.

Edgar Leoni comments: "Since the telescope was not invented until 1610, this would be a prophecy within a prophecy."

And if Nostradamus foresaw the telescope, why should he
not as easily know that Neptune is one of the planets, even
though that orb was not discovered till 1846:

Jupiter joined more to Venus than to the Moon
Appearing with white plenitude:
Venus hidden under the whiteness of Neptune
Struck by Mars by white gravel.

(4.33)

Five years before Nostradamus passed away, Francis Bacon
was born. This giant mind took all knowledge for his province.
His *New Atlantis* anticipates some of our modern inventions.
Before he wrote it, near the end of his career he had anticipated
Sir Isaac Newton by more than fifty years:

The loadstone draws inferior to superior powers as iron in
atoms cleaves to the magnet, but the mass will, like a true
patriot, with appetite of amity" fall towards the center of the
earth.

It may appear odd to many that Shakespeare also seems to
have made this discovery. In Act Four, Scene II of *Troilus and
Cressida,* Cressida exclaims:

But the strong base and building of my love
Is as the very center of the earth,
Drawing all things to it,

37

Is to predict the motor car as remarkable as to "predict" the law of gravity? At any rate, Andrew Jackson Davis, "the seer of Poughkeepsie," did it. In his *Penetralia* published in 1856, he makes several striking prophecies of modern inventions, one being the automobile.

First he asks this question: "Will utilitarianism make any discoveries in locomotive directions?"

Yes, in the almanac language, look out about these days, for carriages and traveling saloons on country roads—sans horses, sans steam, sans any visible motive power, moving with greater speed and safety than at present. Carriages will be moved by a strange and beautiful and simple admixture of aqueous and atmospheric gases—so easily condensed, so simply ignited, and so imparted by a machine somewhat resembling our engines, as to be entirely concealed and manageable between the forward wheels. These vehicles will prevent many embarrassments now experienced by persons living in thinly-populated territories. The first requisite for these land-locomotives will be good roads, upon which, with your engine, without your horses, you may travel with great rapidity.

One is reminded of the ancient Irishman Mac Auliffe's prophecy:

The English tongue will be used by every race,
And a chariot under each foot.

The New Nazis And Afterwards?

Are they? Perhaps. We'd better be careful. Let's not make another mistake.

They call themselves and are called by others the National Democratic Party. They are reputedly conservatives. But the youth section consists of "Young Storm Troopers," "Young Vikings," and "the Ring of Youth." They wear brown shirts, black knickers, buckled belts and peaked caps. Pete Hamill writes in the *New York Post:* "Discipline is enforced according to the old Hitler Youth manual, *The Steel Hat Handbook* of 1927. As part of their training they read the *Last Letter of Hermann Goering.*"

They have had increasing success in local elections. Will they then become a power?

Let us look to Nostradamus to see if they will become important enough for him to describe. There is a prophecy, perhaps two, that may refer to this budding group. The following quatrain has been applied by some to the original Nazis, with woeful incorrectness:

A new sect of philosophers,
Scorning death, gold, honors, and wealth,
Will not limit themselves to the mountains of Germany,
To follow them they will have support and presses.

That the Nazis were *brave* animals, no one will deny. But Nostradamus would not describe them in such positive terms as "scorning death," and they certainly did not scorn gold and wealth, for they were among the greatest looters in history.

Actually the prophecy sounds as though applicable to some German Moral Rearmament movement, but it may refer to the present National Democratic Party of Germany, if it grows much more.

The new movement has elements of the original paganism of the old Nazis. It is likely that the following quatrain refers to the new party:

> In Germany various sects will arise,
> Closely approaching an optimistic paganism,
> The heart captive, and pretty recipes,
> They will return to pay the true tithe.

The "optimistic paganism" may be a reference to the Strength through Joy philosophy of the "Young Vikings," or it may refer to a paganism still to come. But whatever it is, its life will not be too long and it will give way to payment of "the true tithe." The tithe is the tenth paid into the Church, and the *true* tithe would be the payment made to the true Church, Nostradamus, though possibly of Jewish or Israelite ancestry, was a very devout Catholic.

That Germany will become Catholic is also affirmed by the famous Lehnin Prophecy, composed by Nicolaus von Zitzwitz, Abbot of Huysburg in 1692. This prophecy has been remarkably successful, predicting correctly many facts in the history of the ruling house of Brandenburg. But it has something to say about Germany that has not yet come to pass but that well may later in this century:

> The herd will receive its shepherd and Germany her king; the Mark of Brandenburg will forget all her tribulations; she will look to her own and not rejoice over strangers; the roofs of Lehnin and Chorin will rise up again; spirituality (that is, Catholicism) will shine forth again with its one-time splendor, and no wolf will anymore assault the noble sheepfold.

Henry James Forman comments: "Brandenburg is not in the ascendant, nor is Catholicism now triumphing in Germany. Yet it is extraordinary, granting the most direct interpretations, how much has already been fulfilled."

We have clues as to when Germany is to become Catholic: after the debacle of the new Optimistic Paganism Movement and *after* Armageddon, or World War III against the Arab Overlord. Nostradamus writes of a "Trojan blood" hero who sets the Roman Church in Germany on a solid rock foundation *after* his great victories:

> Of Trojan blood will be born a Germanic heart
> Who will become of very high power:
> He will drive out the foreign Arabic people,
> Returning the Church to its pristine pre-eminence.

After the war Germany will allow the Arabs into the country:

> The Holy Empire will come into Germany,
> The Ishmaelites will find open places:
> The asses will want Carmania also,
> The supporters all covered by earth.

Carmania, Leoni explains as "the Persian province at the mouth of the Persian Gulf; or an anagram." The two last lines of the quatrain are ironic. The last-stand Arabs who fought to hold Carmania are dead, "covered with earth." Such is their earthly reward for supporting the Arab Hitler.

The Prophecy Of Fascism

The first seeds of the Second World War were planted years before Benito Mussolini. His modern fascism proved itself the foe of all democracy. Spawned in Milan in 1919, fascism spread to Rome and all Italy, and thence to Germany. In his beginning, Hitler was only an imitation of Mussolini — a despised ape, too — until *Der Fuehrer* became better at autocracy than Il Duce.

The rise of modern fascism was prophesied by Nostradamus four centuries ago, as follows:

> From a little rural domain will rise to the Royal Mount
> One who will tyrannize over vault and finances,
> He will prepare his troop for the Milan march,
> He will exhaust Faenza and Florence of money and men.
>
> (7.32)

Mussolini was born in the "little rural domain" of Dovia, a tiny village of Romagna. He rose to the "Royal Mount" indeed, and here he learned to "tyrannize over vault and finances" by controlling all profits. Precisely, he prepared his troop for the Milan march. The march from Milan was made by fascists, but not by Benito himself. He rode to Rome in the security of a private railway car.

"Faenza and Florence" apparently stand, by synecdoche, for all Italy. That Mussolini exhausted his country of "money and men, " has long been known.

Red China Versus Pink Russia

There exists a remarkable ancient Welsh prophecy, never before given its present interpretation — to my knowledge — it still is in the form of a prophetic dream dreamed by King Arthur. The dream was apparently never fulfilled in his day or in subsequent days up to now, but it still could come to pass.

> In a dream he saw a bear flying in the air, at the noise of which all the shores trembled; also a terrible dragon flying from the west, which enlightened the country with the brightness of its eyes. When these two met, they began a dreadful fight; but the dragon with his fiery breath burned the bear which often assaulted him, and threw him down scorched to the ground. Arthur upon this awaking, related his dream, then those that stood about him, who took upon them to interpret it, told him that the dragon signified himself, but the bear, some giant that should encounter with him.

Those "who took upon them to interpret" the dream, were not necessarily men of vision, and Arthur may not have been the dragon. Observe that these "wise" men cannot begin to interpret the flying bear, except to say it is some giant. A giant nation, perhaps. As for the dragon that also flies, could it be the same that is predicted in the Book of Revelation? St. John sees a great enemy of mankind in "the great red dragon." The dragon is the symbol of China: would not then "the great red dragon" be great Red China? If so, then is not the flying dragon that wounds the bear . . . But finish the interpretation yourself! Let us hope, though, that Arthur's dream was but a dream and nothing more. We should never look upon any evil as inevitable.

Nostradamus And The League Of Nations

When Mussolini was at the peak of his short-lived gala days

he grew bold and took Ethiopia; Hitler took the Rhineland. The world looked on in fearful awe, heartsick. The League of Nations made many protests. Many statesmen pinned their hopes on these speeches, hoping they would lead to action. But Nostradamus had written:

> The sermons from Geneva will vex,
> Days will grow into weeks,
> Then months, then years, then all will fail,
> The magistrates will condemn their vain laws.

(1.47)

Some interpreters have thought this quatrain a prophecy of John Calvin's New Religious Order in Geneva. Possibly. But even the skeptical Leoni believes the quatrain much better fits the failure of the League of Nations.

Another prophecy of Nostradamus concerns the same failure of the League, a prophecy that is so clear as to need no interpretation:

> Because of the Germans,
> They and their neighbors around them
> Will be in wars for control of the clouds...
> The shortcomings of Geneva will be laid bare.

Prophecy On The Coming Of Communism

More than a century ago, Heinrich Heine, German-Jewish poet and friend of Karl Marx, made an astonishingly accurate prophecy. In 1834, he wrote:

> Communism is the secret name of the dread antagonist setting proletarian rule with all its consequences against the present bourgeois regime. It will be a frightful duel. How will it end? No one knows but gods and goddesses acquainted with the future. We only know this much: Communism, though little discussed now and loitering in hidden garrets on miserable straw pallets, is the dark hero destined for a great, if temporary, role in the modern tragedy...

> It would be war, the ghastliest war of destruction — which would unfortunately call the two noblest nations of civilization into the arena, to the ruin of both: France and Germany. England, the great sea serpent always able to crawl back into its vast watery lair, and Russia, which also has the safest hiding places in its vast fir forests, steppes and icy wastes — these two, in a normal political war, cannot be annihilated even by the most crushing defeats. But Germany is far more menaced in such cases, and France in particular could lose her political existence in the most pitiful manner.

> That, however, would only be the first act of the great melodrama, the prologue, as it were. The second act is the European and the World Revolution, the great duel between the destitute and the aristocracy of wealth; and in that there will be no mention of either nationality or religion: there will be only one fatherland, the globe, and only one faith, that in happiness on Earth. Will the religious doctrines of the past rise in all countries, in desperate resistance — and will perhaps this attempt constitute the third act? Will the old absolutist tradition enter the stage, though in a new costume and with new cues and slogans? How

could that drama end?

I do not know; but I think that eventually the great sea serpent will have its head crushed, and the skin of the Northern bear will be pulled over his ears. There may be only one flock then and one shepherd — one free shepherd with an iron staff, and a shorn-alike, bleating-alike human herd!

Wild, gloomy times are roaring toward us, and a prophet wishing to write a new apocalypse would have to invent entirely new beasts so terrible that St. John's older animal symbols would be like gentle doves and cupids in comparison. The gods are veiling their faces in pity on the children of man, their long-time charges, and perhaps over their own fate. The future smells of Russian leather, blood, godlessness, and many whippings. I should advise our grandchildren to be born with very thick skin on their backs.

Reading this prophecy inclines one to the belief that Heine had a genuinely psychic ability to foresee the future. After all, it is no mean judgment to be able in the year 1834 to associate a coming and overwhelmingly powerful communism with godlessness and Russian leather. The prophecy made no sense in his day; but we all understand it today.

Prophecies Of Things To Come

Fez Will Be News

Two brewing prophecies of Nostradamus to be fulfilled in this century concern Fez, chief city of Morocco, formerly its capital. The first concerns an early morning rebellion against the king of Morocco, resulting in his over-throw:

At daybreak at the second cockcrow,
Those of Tunis, of Fez, and of Bugiah;
The King of Morocco taken captive by the Arabs,
The year 1607 from the Liturgy.

Au point du jour au second chant du coq,
Ceux de Tunes, de Fez, et de Bugie,
Par les Arabes captif le Roi Maroq,
L'an mil six cent et sept, de Liturgie. (6.54)

Problem: to find the predicted year of fulfillment. Rolfe Boswell, interpreting this quatrain in a book published in the forties believed the fulfillment date was 1981. He surmised the liturgy referred to was that of Auxentius, Bishop of Milan, the possible terminal date for whose liturgy could have been 374 A. D.

Professor John Warwick Montgomery tried to help me here, but he remarked there were many liturgies around in Nostradamus' days and it would be difficult to know which were important to him. My suggestion here is that possibly close to fulfillment time a specific liturgy will be in the news for some reason, and the date of this, added to 1607 will be revelatory.

Morocco and Libya recently signed a treaty to establish a

union of states, which forsees a union that will include Algeria (Bugiah is in Algeria) and Tunisia. King Hassan II and Khadafy signed the accord at Oujda on the Morocco-Algeria border.

The other "Fez" prophecy is for a somewhat later time:

From Fez the reign will reach out to those of Europe,
Their city on fire, and blade will slash:
The great one of Asia, land and sea, with great troop,
He will drive to death blues, blue-greens, the cross.

De Fez le regne parviendra á ceux d'Europe,
Few leur cité, et lame tranchera:
Le grand d'Asie terre et mer a grande troupe,
Que bleus, pers, croix a mort déchassera. (6.90)

The Great One of Asia may be the king of terror predicted in the 1999 prophecy. Is he in league with the Arab conqueror? A German leader is to drive the Arabs out of Germany and a French King Henry ditto out of France. Apparently Fez is the Arab empire's springboard to Europe.

The Great Motor Renews The Ages

In 1982, an article in a tabloid newspaper described a new electrical engine that returns most of its power to its batteries and "that can change history by 1984." Stupendous, if so. Here is an engine, apparently, that may force mankind to revise and rewrite some of the laws of physics, utterly revolutionary in principle, that creates and endlessly recycles electrical energy, that can replace gasoline engines in motorcars, thereby ending most pollution, that will enable homes to supply their own electricity "forever" for a $200 investment, that can end the need for dangerous atomic reactor plants, and so on.

As I began to realize the implications of this revolutionary invention, there began to jingle in my mind a line in a prophecy of Nostradamus. The line reads:

The great motor renews the ages.

And the entire quatrain, as it appeared in my *Prophecies on World Events*:

After a great human exhaustion a greater makes ready,
The great motor renovates the centuries:
Plague, blood, milk, famine, iron and pestilence,
In the sky fire seen, long running spark.

(II.46)

At the time I recalled *Life* Magazine's photographs of Sputnik, and around the same time the discovery in England of contaminated milk.

The first line is not hopeful for humanity. If the great age-renewing motor is the one recently described, we are in for a greater exhaustion than World War Two. But if the great motor is atomic fission, then World War Two was the greater of two exhaustions. It would be strange if something as important as atomic power were not pre-recorded by Nostradamus, so let us be hopeful of good.

According to St. Odile, after the Hitler War, "the sun will shine with a new and glorious radiance." However, how long after?

Two Prophecies On the Arctic Pole

A quatrain of Nostradamus that conceivably may soon be of current interest reads:

When those of the Arctic pole are united together,
In the East great terror and fear:
The newly elected, sustained the great one trembles,
Rhodes, Constantinople stained with barbarian blood.

(VI,21)

Quand ceux du pole arctique unis ensemble,
En Orient grand effrayeur et crainte:
Elu nouveau, soutenu le grand tremble,
Rodes, Bisance de sang Barbare teinte.

With no intention of asserting that I know its meaning, or whether or not it will soon be fulfilled, it does look like a "latter-day" prophecy. The reader may tussle with it.

Be careful of the word *Orient*. To Nostradamus, it means *Middle*, not *Far East*. For him the Far East is Asia. As for *barbare*, he pens it for Arabs on the war-path. None of any of this may apply today; but if Russia and the U.S.A. unite to constitute a world-police-force for peace the picture could change overnight.

Such a police force, run by two giants with atomic powers of persuasion would cause almost uncontrollable consternation throughout the entire Middle East. This may happen at a time when a newly-elected successor to Andropov or a successor's successor appears on the scene.

Another quatrain also concerns the Arctic pole. It sounds like a science-fiction account of a future happening — but not too unlikely a fiction:

> Very great famine by pestiferous wave,
> By long rain the length of the Arctic pole:
> Samarobryn hundred leagues from the hemisphere,
> They will live without law exempt from politics.

(VI,5)

> *Si grande famine par onde pestifere,*
> *Par Pluie longue le long du Pole arctique:*
> *Samarobryn cent lieus de l'hémisphere,*
> *Vivront sans loi exempt de politique.*

Edgar Leoni, possibly facetiously, suggests that Nostradamus may be not altogether correctly hearing the name of a spacestation astronaut Sam R. O'Brian! Who can say? Nostradamus on a surprising number of occasions does predict the actual names of historical figures not yet born when his pen moved.

Leoni's fuller comment on this quatrain is better than good. He writes:

> Of all the prophecies of Nostradamus, there is probably none more completely inapplicable to his own period, or to the whole four centuries to the 1960's than this one. Suddenly, it has an excellent chance of a very impressive fulfillment. A league was generally about 2.5 miles, sometimes as much as 4.5 miles . . . Now, there is only one way one can get 270 miles from the hemisphere, and this is upwards into space. And note that there is real meaning to "hemisphere," since anyone a certain distance away from merely the "earth" on one side would be many times that distance away from the other side of the earth at any given moment . . . might we not have a prophecy of a space-station thought by Nostradamus, rightly or wrongly, to be about 270 miles from the earthly hemisphere? . . .
>
> In addition to the space reference we have cryptic references to other matters sounding rather contemporary: activity in the

Arctic of a strange sort in line 2, and in line 1 perhaps a bit of bacteriological warfare.

The Sam Rayburn

Recently, a Mr. Timothly Evans, a representative of DBA Communications came to my house to discuss the possibility of my doing a Nostradamus documentary for HBO. I gave him a copy of my newly-published *Nostradamus And The End Of Evil*. A few days later he sent me a most remarkable letter, together with a photocopy of the Poseidon Submarine. He writes:

> You might find this fact interesting. In reading the first edition of your "End of Evils Begun", I paid little attention to the quatrain which mentioned "Samarobryn" until I ran across the enclosed picture of the nuclear submarine "U.S.S. Sam Rayburn." This submarine is part of the fleet that patrols the North Atlantic and its missiles would indeed travel across the Arctic Circle. I can't think of a more "pestiferous wave" than that caused by a submarine-launched nuclear missile. As for the "hundred leagues from the hemisphere" I don't have the mathematics capability to figure the height of the missile's trajectory, though its range is from 2500 to 3200 miles. Of course, it's hard to determine what Nostradamus is speaking about till after the fact, but I indeed hope he was foreseeing an astronaut named "Sam R. O'Brian" and not a nuclear submarine attack.

It is certainly possible, as Timothy Evans has suggested, that *Samarobryn* is meant for *Sam Rayburn*.

Read aloud one after the other. Thus:

SamaRobryn

Sam Rayburn

Leoni may have triggered something. He heard the name *Sam* in it.

Equally remarkably, *Samarobryn* may also be *an anagram* for *Sam Rayburn*. Nostradamus, because he lived when he did, made use of anagrams. The poets of his day loved them.

According to the *Dictionnaire de Trévoux* a one-letter change was allowable in making an anagram.

Now, take the first three letters of *Sam Rayburn*, that is, *Sam*. This leaves *Arobryn*. Now take out *Ray*. This leaves *Obrn*.

Thus you have *Born*, which, with the allowed one-letter change yields *Burn* and the anagram is perfect for *Sam Rayburn*.

Leoni thought to place his *Sam* in a space-station about 270 miles above the hemisphere. This would be perfect if our government were to dub a space-station with that same name of Rayburn—which is not beyond possibility.

But, might we not have, instead of a 270 mile up space-tation a submarine capable of shooting a nuclear-powered missile with a trajectory apogee of 270 miles? "They will live without law, exempt from politics" could apply to men biding their time in the *U.S.S. Sam Rayburn*.

The Nostradamus line just quoted applies beautifully to men of war living in a submarine. Indeed, when I quoted the prophecy to a friend who had spent nine days aboard a submarine, he described his experience in these words:

"In a ship the captain is the sole on-board authority, especially when one is totally out of sight of land—such as is especially true in a submarine. You have almost total isolation. Before a week goes by one forgets that another world exists. There is no night or day, only a constant electric light. After being on board a few days I was walking down the passageway adjacent to the radio room and was quite surprised to find news bulletins describing events happening in New York, London, Paris and elsewhere, and had to put my mind back to say, 'Yes, indeed, there is another world out there.' "

Now what about line three of the quatrain: "a hundred leagues from the hemisphere"? It may be that instead of Nostradamus having predicted a space-station 270 miles or so above the hemisphere he may have intended instead a submarine station from which is shot a missile with a trajectory of 270 miles or so from the hemisphere.

To check, I phoned Rockwell International, in Fullerton, and learned indeed from a good authority that though 270 miles is rather high, the missile could indeed push that far up and no doubt sometimes would.

Three heads are better than one. The coincidences are remarkable. And possibly Edgar Leoni had a genuine psychic insight when he suggested that *Samarobryn* might be *Sam R. O'Brian*.

And in turn, his hunch suggested to Timothy Evans his

own hunch:
   Sam Rayburn.

What Can We Do About It?

Here is a terrible disaster predicted. Perhaps a button is pushed by accident, perhaps on purpose. The result is a "pestiferous wave" which brings in its wake famine. Is that the universal famine found in another quatrain?

Can we do anything to prevent this major evil? Yes. First: prayer; second: prayer; third: prayer. A forecast evil that has not yet happened is not inevitable. Nostradamus knew this. The Bible prophets knew this. So expect good, But let the prophecy serve as a warning.

So, keep an eye on the *Sam Rayburn* submarine. Is there something about it that makes it especially dangerous? Find out if this is so. And make sure the eyes around it are eagle.

Pray against the prophecy's fulfillment. Here we have a warning of a cataclysmic disaster we may specifically ward off through that Infinite Power which is both all around us . . . and ours.

There is fair agreement among Nostradamians that the following quatrain concerns our New World:

From the aquatic triplicity will be born
One who will make Thursday his holiday:
His fame, praise, rule and puissance will grow,
By land and sea tempest in the East.

(I,50)

De l'aquatique Triplicité nâitra
D'un qui fera le jeudi pour sa fête:
Son Bruit, los, regne, sa puissance croîtra,
Par terre et mer aux Orients tempête.

America may be meant. We have three seas, and Thursday is our Thanksgiving. Our power is not yet at peak, but when it comes—in a time of world turmoil—there may well be tempest in the East by land and sea.

If the Thursday holiday prophecy has *not* yet come to pass, the following quatrain may refer to an extraordinary event:

The earth and the air will freeze very great water,

When one comes to honor Thursday:
That which will be was never so beautiful,
From the four corners they will come to honor it.

(X,71)

La terre et l'air geleront si grand eau,
Lorsqu'on viendra pour Jeudi vénérer:
Ce que sera jamais ne fut si beau,
Des quatres parts les viendront honorer.

The interpretation of this I leave to the reader. If both predictions relate to one and the same time-period, Thursday will have more significance than does our present Thanksgiving. Some new and ingenious science-fiction-type invention seems suggested.

A quatrain frequently misunderstood and therefore misinterpreted reads:

The man from the East will leave his seat,
To pass the Apennine mountains to see France;
He will pierce through the sky, the waters and snow,
And will strike everyone with his rod.

(II,29)

L'Oriental sortira de son siège,
Passer les monts Apennins voir la Gaule;
Transpercera le ciel, les eaux et neige,
Et un chacun frappera de sa gaule.

The error made is in translating *Oriental* as Oriental. Nostradamus simply means Easterner, or man from the East. And East means *Middle* East, not *Far* East. When Nostradamus intends the Far East he usually writes Asia.

One Nostradamian, misinterpreting the above prophecy, writes: "The Chinese forces, eager for their share of Europe, will take part in the assault on France. The same Oriental leader who attacked southern Russia and Turkey at the beginning of the war will now travel further to the west, bringing his forces by air and sea and via the mountains, using his terrible rod-shaped weapon to spread terror and death wherever he goes."

Not that China may not be a part of this situation, but it is not stated in this prophecy. Another quatrain, however, may indicate something of the sort. Edgar Leoni thinks it possible that *Angolmois,* in the 1999 prophecy, is an anagram of Mongolois. In which case "the great King of Angolmois" would be the "great Mongol king." And "to revive the great Mongol King" would mean something like reviving the days of that Asiatic Hitler Ghenghis Khan.

The same Mongol war-lord may be referred to in another quatrain, which in turn may be a sequel to the "King of Morocco . . . taken by the Arabs" quatrain, a prophecy to be fulfilled in this century.

> From Fez the reign will come to those of Europe,
> Their city on fire, and blade will slash:
> The great man of Asia land and sea with great army,
> So that blues, grays, and of the cross chased to death.
>
> (VI, 80)
>
> *De Fez le regne parviendra à ceus d'Europe,*
> *Feu leur cité, et lame tranchera:*
> *Le grand d'Asie terre et mer à grande troupe,*
> *Que bleus, pers, croix à mort déchassera.*

Turning now to a quatrain already briefly commented on elsewhere in this book in a chapter entitled *A World Conqueror from Arabia?* I note how that *Orient* is not the English Orient but *East.* Asia, however, is also mentioned. Could there then be two antichrists, one from the Far and the other from the Middle East? Time will tell.

> The one so long awaited will never come again,
> He will appear into Europe and in Asia,
> One issued from the line of the great Hermes,
> And he will grow above all the kings of the East.
>
> (X,75)
>
> *Tant attendu, ne reviendra jamais,*
> *Dedans l'Europe en Asie paraitra,*
> *Un de le ligne yssu du grand Hermes,*
> *Et sur touts roys des Orients croistra.*

The first line seems to suggest that what is popularly called "the Second Coming" will not take place in *human* form. Whether this was a conviction of Nostradamus or not cannot be determined; but he was a very devout Catholic and, with his learning, no doubt knew the Catholic Church Fathers well. And they did not believe the Second Coming meant the return appearance of a thirty-three year old Jesus scheduled to step on to a literal royal throne in Jerusalem and for a thousand years judge from that throne murderers, child molesters, wife-beaters, slithery politicians, military men of massacre, assorted evil- doers, with all the etceteras.

The second line of the quatrain, however, indicates that someone of momentous importance is to come in earthly form. Ironically, it sounds like an antichrist. We wait for Christ and get instead a flagellator. But this may precede the authentic Second Coming, however that glorious event is interpreted.

The Doom of Germany Under Hitler

In the latter years of the seventh century a little girl was born blind in the palace of great Lord Adalric of Alsace. He was a hard man and refused to have anything to do with his daughter, so she was turned over to the nuns. As years passed, the child "throve under the heavens" and grew into a beautiful character. The story goes that at last a miracle was performed on her. A visiting Bishop of Ratisbon healed her of her blindness. The holy man bestowed on her the name "Odile," which means "Daughter of Light." He named her well, as she was no longer of the darkness or of the night. And now her relenting father, abashed yet proud, invited her back to his ancestral castle. of Hohenburg. Yes, she said—she would come, but on one condition: that her father turn the castle into a nunnery. And henceforth, here on the heights of Hohenburg she lived out her days in piety and good works, ever after to be known as the patron saint of Alsace.

To this holy maid a wondrous prophecy has been attributed, a Latin prose-poem on the recent Hitler war. Some critics have questioned her authorship of the work, saying that perhaps it was written by a modest monk, who not wishing to sign his name to it, dedicated it instead to "the Daughter of Light" who is the patroness of prophecy. But that is conjecture. The wonderful work is probably her own. And what matters most about it is that it was certainly written centuries before Der Fuehrer began to cast his ugly shadow over Earth. That is, this masterpiece of prophecy is unquestionably an authentic vision, so amazing, so perfect and circumstantial in its details—imperfect only in time-intervals (which are always hardest for a prophet to get)—that some who read it may think it a gigantic hoax perpetrated after the event.

At any rate, here it is in its entirety in a literal translation and with a running commentary where necessary:

> Listen, listen, O my brother, for I have seen the trembling of the forests and the mountains. The nations are in a stupor, for never in any place in the universe has like perturbation been witnessed.

(The nations are in a stupor. This was truer of World War II than of any previous wars. Hitler conquered the little nations one by one, hypnotizing them as a snake does a bird, petrifying them with a fear which prevented their acting until it was too late. And his fifth columnists helped the stupor of the nations.)

Stanley High, in an article entitled "Hitler's Ersatz Religion," reprinted in the *Reader's Digest*, wrote:

> The whole power of the (Nazi) party is behind the effort to uproot Christianity and substitute for it a heathen tribalism. Instruction in the new faith is part of all teachers' training courses, its literature is required reading in the schools. The daily press and the movies are required to propagate the faith; its hymn book has been bought by more than 1,000,000 German families . . . Frequently, Hitler is spoken of as 'Our Redeemer.' The famous Christian hymn, *Christ, Thou Lord of the New Age,* has been changed for party gatherings to *Hitler, Thou Lord of the New Age* . . .
>
> In many government orphanages a prayer to Hitler is required of the children before every meal: "To Thee I owe, alone, my daily bread; abandon thou me never, with me for'er abide, Fuehrer, my Fuehrer, my Faith and my Light. . . ."
>
> The Minister of the Interior warns German parents that names taken from the Bible or names of saints or Christian martyrs will no longer be accepted by the state. . . Christmas, solemnly affirm the Nazi researchers, did not originate with Christ at all. It originated with Wotan—a 100 per cent German god and one of the first and greatest Nazis. . . . Good Friday is dedicated to Baldur—another one of Nazism's mythological forebears. "The soldier," says a Nazi educator, "who throws his last hand grenade, the dying seaman who pronounces the Fuehrer's name as his last word, these are, for us, divine figures much more than the crucified Jew."

The National song of Nazi Germany, is the Horst Wessel

lied. Wessel was a young National Socialist who made a living by renting out whores and was finally killed in a brawl over one of them. Yet he was the hero of the young Nazis and of the whole German nation. Their songs contained such lines as: "We follow not Christ but Horst Wessel. . . . I am no Christian and no Catholic . . . The Church can take a running jump!"

Saint Odile was right: Hitler was an Antichrist from every facet looked at, from every pore of his being.

Observe how the saint predicts that the German tyrant will make Rachel weep Rachel is a Jewish name, and the greatest sufferers of all under the Antichrist were the Jews).

The conqueror will come from the banks of the Danube.

(Hitler came from the Danubian state of Austria, and was born near the river's banks.)

The time is arrived when Germany will be called the most warlike-loving nation on Earth.

As far back as the time of Caesar and Tacitus, Germany was notorious for her cruelty and warlikeness. Her literature expresses through countless writers the idea of world domination. Nietzsche, perhaps Germany's "greatest" writer, wrote to his people, "Ye shall love peace—as a means to new wars, and a short peace better than a long one." Bernhardi proclaimed with pride, "We Germans are the most warlike nation in the world." A hundred years ago the German-Jewish poet Heinrich Heine prophesied, "In the past Christianity has, to a certain extent, moderated the German delight in war. But once the charm that tames it, the cross, is broken, the savagery of those old warriors will burst forth anew . . . and when you hear a crash such as the world has never heard before, you will know 'The German thunder has found its mark.' "

The time is arrived when there will spring from her womb the terrible man who will undertake the world-war, and whom men under arms will call "Antichrist." He who will be damned by mothers in thousands, as they cry like Rachel for their children, and refuse consolation because their children no longer live, and because all will have been laid waste in their homes.

Hitler was a true Antichrist not only in tyranny and cruelty, but in his opposition to, and hatred of, Christianity itself, which papers found by the Allied Command after the war proved beyond doubt, for in them were detailed plans for the systematic extirpation of all organized Christianity—not merely Catholic Christianity. The Fuehrer's open hatred of the teachings of Jesus should have been evident to many to whom it was not. Hitler openly espoused the philosophy of Nietzsche, and was once photographed beside a statue of this firebrand writer. Nazi soldiers were provided with pocket editions of selections from his works, much as the Allied soldiers are provided with Bibles. There is no doubt as to the violent anti-Christianity of the man whose writings were so loved by the Nazis. Take the following consistent passages culled from his works: "Christianity is fit for only old women and children."

"How a German can even feel Christian is more than I can understand."

"If humanity never gets rid of Christianity the Germans will be to blame."

"Every other book becomes clean after one reads the New Testament."

"The New Testament is filthy."

"I am Antichrist."

"My task—one of the greatest that man could take upon himself—is to exterminate Christianity."

He will be a remarkable leader among men. The war he has undertaken is the most terrifying humans have ever undergone—in the height of the mountains. His arms will be flaming . . .

Flame-throwing tanks and other fiery horrors were used by the Germans in the Battle of France.

. . . And the helmets of his soldiers are in the midst of bristling, shining weapons, while their hands brandish flaming torches. How many of the dead lie here!

He will win victories on land and sea, and even in the air; and I see his war-skilled winged warriors, riding up with a clattering noise into the clouds, there seizing stars to throw them down on the cities of the world, lighting gigantic fires.

This remarkable prediction of air warfare is perhaps even more surprising in the original Latin:

Videoque viros belli artibus claros et pennatos, qui in

oequitationibus terricrepis ad nubes advolant, stellas capientes et dejicientes in urbes universi orbis ut comburant igne altissimo.

Even a hundred years ago these lines would not have made sense. Today they do perfectly.

At that there is consternation among the nations, who exclaim: "Whence comes his strength! How has he been able to undertake such a war!"

Exactly what all the world said while watching the course of Hitler's conquests.

The Earth will seem overturned by the collision of armies. Rivers of blood will seem to flow. In the depths of the sea the monsters will be stunned by the conflagration . . .
(Depth bombs have done this.)
While black tempests will lay all waste. Future generations will be astonished that his enemies were not able to hold back the march of his mighty victories.
And the war will be long, and the victor will have attained the height of his triumphs about the middle of the sixth month of the second year of the war.

This specific statement terminates the "terrible man's" triumphs in March-April, 1941, America passed the Lend-Lease Bill, at which isolationists held up their hands in horror, exclaiming, "Now we are committed to the defeat of Hitler!" But even more important, Schickelgruber's conquests ended in the period prophesied. In April he took Jugo-Slavia and helped Mussolini conquer Greece, but this was Der Fuehrer's last successful front. His next front was Russia, where he was a miserable failure.

This will be the end of the period called that of bloody victories.
The jeering leader will cry, "Accept my yoke!". . .
(An accurate description of the notorious "peace offensives").
. . . But they will not accept it—and the war will go on. And he will cry: "Woe to them, for I am their conqueror!"
(A good description of the typical Hitler ratings).
The second part of the war will equal in length half the first period. It will be known as the period of decline.

March to December, 1941. In the latter month even the most pessimistic were able to see signs of deterioration within the Nazi Empire. The great retreat—or rather rout—had begun in Russia, and to cap all, America entered the war, a tremendous blow to Naziland in every way.

It will be full of unexpected things . . .

Probably no war in history has been so full of surprises as World War Part Two. And Hitler relied on the blitzbrieg to achieve his ends.

It will be full of unexpected things that will cause the peoples of the world to quake, particularly when twenty nations and adverse peoples have been swept into the war.

The Germans believed in literal world-rule by war, and by tyranny in peace. All must submit to them, whether as foes or allies. The holy maid described the German conqueror as "the terrible man who will undertake war on the world." True. Hitler had no willing allies, as he was the enemy of the whole human race.

A *New York Herald Tribune* headline for June 23, 1941 read:

German Army Now In Nineteen Foreign Lands
Berlin, June 22 (AP).—Assuming that the German Army was on Russian soil, the Nazi forces were in 19 foreign countries today, in some as allies, and in some as conquerors.
Besides Russia, they are Poland, Denmark, Norway, Belgium, Holland, France, Luxembourg, Hungary, Rumania, Bulgaria, Yugoslavia, Greece, Slovakia, Bohemia, Finland, Croatia, Italy, and Egypt.

Britain is not included in the list, because she was not invaded. But she was in the war, hence by actual count, Russia was the twentieth nation to find herself opposing Hitler. Did the world quake then!

About the middle of the period of decline the sorrowful cities of the leader will cry: "Let us have peace, let us have peace!" But no peace will be given them.
It will not be the end of these wars, but a certain end, when there is hand to hand fighting in the citadel of citadels.

In his address to the Canadian Parliament in December,

1941, Prime Minister Churchill promised "an assault upon the citadels and homelands of the guilty powers, both in Europe and in Asia." The "citadel of citadels" of the prophecy would be Berlin, the chief city of the conqueror. The following Associated Press Report is interesting:

London, Jan. 8. — "Evidently expecting trouble" in the form of a possible army coup against the Hitler Government, Nazi officials in Berlin have erected machine-gun posts at all key points of the city, the military correspondent of the *London Daily Express* reported today . . .

"With the real magnitude of the German reverses and casualties in Russia filtering into the Reich, and America's entry increasing German anxieties, Hitler is 'evidently expecting trouble,' "

Then some of the women of his country will be of troubled mind, and would like to stone him.

On one occasion, according to a news report, German women crowded in front of a railway track to prevent a troop train of German soldiers from departing. A March 30, 1942 UP report from Moscow read in part: "The announcement of a reduction of bread rations in Germany two weeks ago caused riots in Cologne, Chemnitz and Dusseldorf, and Nazi Storm Troopers fired into a crowd of women in another city when they demanded bread for their children, Tass the official Soviet news agency, said today.".

But many prodigies will take place in the Orient also.

This is the last event mentioned by Saint Odile as taking place in the second period, which ends December, 1941. No comment is necessary on what happened on this month and year.

Now has come the short period, called the time of invasion . . .

This means that the rout of the German troops, which began in December, is to continue until the Russians reach Berlin and beyond. Note how accurately the prophet has timed this period: Prime Minister Churchill said, on December 30, 1941, "The tide has turned against the Hun.".

And the conqueror will be in a state of confusion concerning his men.

On December 22, 1941, our newspapers reported in big head-lines that Adolph Hitler had taken over supreme command of the German Army. This was an astonishing action, as von Brauchitsch had for more than two years been identified with all its stupendous successes. *Time* magazine for January 5, 1942, commented:

> It was an uneasy New Year for Adolf Hitler. Something was rotten in the German Army . . . This is the roughly consistent story: Last fall Field Marshal von Brauchitsch had advised dig-ging in for the Russian winter. Adolf Hitler had insisted on Maintaining a double offensive against Moscow and the Caucasus. More recently, since the failure of his Russian designs, Hitler has proposed a turnabout invasion of Britain. This had been opposed by all his top commanders, all proud veterans of German's aristocratic military caste—Field Marshals von Brauchitsch, Feder von Bock, Ritter Wilhelm von Leeb, Gerd von Rundstedt. They had now been dismissed or "resigned" or were "gravely ill."
>
> His feud with the Army had become widespread gossip, not only in Germany, but elsewhere.

Note how precise Saint Odile is in assigning this event to the beginning of the third period, i.e., December, 1941-January, 1941.

> And for the justice of things his land, because impious and unjust, will suffer devastation in all parts. Around the mountain there will be vast horrors of human blood in the last battle, and I see the nations in the temple of the Lord giving thanks for their deliverance. For there has appeared the leader of leaders by whom they will live to victory.

A fitting description of General Eisenhower, who was made supreme commander of all the Allied Forces and who led the Great Invasion.

> A great disease, which the men have not known, will deci-mate the troops of the conqueror, and people will say to each other: "This is the finger of God; this is punishment for crime."

One December 16, 1941—again note the date—the *New York Herald Tribune* gave this welcome news:

Wave Of Typhus Called Threat To German Army

... A British broadcast heard by the Columbia Broadcasting System described the epidemics as a 'new and terrible enemy threatening Hitler's army from the rear' and said thousands had fallen victim in Vilna, Bialystok, Brest-Litovsk and Minsk.

On January 13, 1942, a follow-up headline in the *Herald Tribune read:*

Nazis Rushing Doctors To Stem Typhus At Front

The prophecy continues inexorably:

They will say his end is near when the scepter is no longer in his hands, and my people will rejoice.

For God is just, even though patient with the fierceness of perturbations and hardness of heart. Not all the nations will remain despoiled who have believed in Him, and they will receive something further in this world.

Innumerable places, in which all was laid waste in blood and flames, will be unexpectedly saved by the divine gift which comes from the human army.

One wonders if the atomic bomb, which brought World War Two to a close with greater speed than would have happened without it, could rightly be called a blessing. I doubt if the Saint would so have seen it. The bombing of Hiroshima was a crime. Then, what the divine gift was, it is hard to ascertain. Perhaps the growing strength of the Allies, enabling them to conquer the predicted Antichrist.

The region of Lutetia, whose future devastation the nations will have believed in, will be providentially saved, on account of the holy hills and devout women.

Though many cities were devastated from the air in the Hitler war—including world capitals—Lutetia, as Paris was once known, was saved.

They will ascend the mountain and offer thanks to God, saying: "Do not hold this sin against them, that this desolation should befall another time."

We did not thank and pray thus after the first World

Holocaust as we did in the second. There were more prayers, prayers that there be no third "war to end war".

But woe in these days to those in whom is no fear of the Antichrist; for he is the father of those whose doom will come.

The prediction was fulfilled: woe came to those who believed they could do business with Hitler! Woe came to the Lavals, the Quislings, and other traitors!

Therefore many more tears will be shed!

Woe came to the guilty when the prison camps were opened. The mills of the gods ground slowly, but finely and finally. Late were the Nuremburg trials and the execution of Eichman, but not too late.

For the time has come when men will rejoice on account of peace under the sword.

What a strange prediction, that mankind will actually rejoice and be glad to live in a "peace under the sword." Yet what better way does man know of feeling somewhat secure from threat of future Hitlers.

And they will see the two horns of the moon join the cross.

Towards the close of the war Turkey, whose symbol is the Mohammedan crescent moon, joined forces with the Western Powers.

In these days frightened men will really worship God, and the sun will shine with a very new and glorious radiance.

So concludes this wonderful vision, a prophecy ninety percent correct, correct in its depiction of the entire course of World War Two, inapplicable to any other war in history, even World War One; correct in its events and their sequence, incorrect only only in its shortening of the third period of the war. Hitler scored his last major triumphs exactly within the prophesied time. And Saint Odile's first period enclosed all of Hitler's peace offensives. And the decline set in as the Saint said. In this period the twentieth nation was to become involved in the holocaust, and so it did. At the end of this period there were to be "many prodigies in the Orient," and the end came in

December, 1941. December, too, was to mark the turn of the tide, which would start with the conqueror's confusion over his warriors. It was in December that sober, realistic Churchill affirmed, "The tide has turned against the Hun," and this same month Der Fuehrer took over the supreme command of his army. The typhus, too, took its toll within this third and final period.

Now, to make the remarkable quality of this seventh century prophecy seeable at a glance, here follows an outline of the vision, in chronological sequence:

Outline Of The Prophecy

Time for fulfillment: When Germany becomes most warlike nation in the world.

Character of the Conqueror: Terrible man, known as an Antichrist. Will come from banks of Danube. Will wage war on world. Remarkable leader among men.

Character of the war: A world war, started by brutal German conqueror. Most terrifying war ever known. Full of surprises. Flaming weapons used by conqueror. Great cities set on fire by his flying warriors. Terrible sea battles affecting even the depths. The nations stunned, and astonished at German conqueror's military strength. "How has he been able to undertake such a war?"

Saint Odile's Chronology of Events

The First Period (About 18 months: Conqueror at peak of triumphs at end of this period. He makes peace offensives, belligerent, threatening.

The Second Period (9 months): Conqueror's power on decline in this period. Great surprise when 20 opposing nations have entered war. World to shake at this. "Women of troubled mind would like to stone him." "Many prodigies in Orient also."

The Period of Invasion (Short period, according to the prophecy. This "short" third period proved to be considerably longer than the prophet believed or the world wished, but the events within the period were correctly predicted, and in correct sequence. As is seen here.): "Victor confused concerning his men." "Leader of leaders will rout conqueror's troops." German warriors "decimated by great disease." "Hand to hand fighting in the citadel of citadels." Germany invaded. Paris saved. "Woe to those who fear not AntiChrist." "Peace under the sword." Crescent joins Cross. "Sun shines with new and glorious radiance."

Now for a chronological outline of the actually fulfilled events:

The First Period (September 1939 to March-April, 1941): March 7, 1941, Lend-Lease bill passed, committing America to defeat of Hitler. April, 1941, Yugoslavia and Greece Hitler's last major victories. Next front Russia, a miserable failure for Der Fuehrer. All notorious peace offensives took place in this period.

The Second Period (March 1941, to December 1941): Russia twentieth nation to find itself opposing Hitler, who attacked by surprise. German women stopped railway trains. December 7, 1941, Japan attacks Pearl Harbor. (Note that Saint Odile places this as last event of second period). December 1941, German rout begins. Tide has turned.

The Period of Invasion (dates from December, 1941): December 22, 1941, Hitler takes over supreme command of untrustworthy Army. From this time on his most important generals dismissed, have heart failure, die, etc., etc. General Eisenhower made "leader of leaders." December 16, 1941, "Wave of Typhus called threat to German Army." January 13, 1942, "Nazis rushing doctors to stem typhus at front."

In my 1942-published pamphlet on the present prophecy, I was able, thanks to the clearness of Odile's vision, to write correctly of the then future course of the war. I wrote:

"Paris will have been saved."
"Rout by Russians to continue until Berlin reached."
"Laval and Quisling yet unpunished."
"Moslem power still at odds with Britain in Indian issue—or does Crescent here refer to Turkey joining forces leagued against the Antichrist?"

The Secret of Prophecy

An illuminating conversation between an interpreter of Nostradamus and skeptic, in which the great seer's gifts are proven and explained. You, too, can interpret him.

Interpreter: prophecy is a scientific fact, and Nostradamus is an authentic prophet.

Skeptic: I doubt it. I've seen his prophecies quoted in the newspapers, and I can't say they impressed me.

I: I don't blame you. If I had read only the newspaper articles on the prophet I would probably think as you do. Most of those articles were written for readers who are interested, not in a scientific study of prophecy, but in the future. And the future is debatable.

Nostradamus carries his prophecies up to the year 3797, so there are many of his predictions that have not been unraveled. The mistake is made when inexpert commentators try to unravel them *before* the event. This can seldom be done. It can only be done when there is a sufficiency of interrelated prophecies which cast mutual light on one another, or when we are so near the event prophesied that we may find a clear clue to go by. Otherwise, until the event overtakes the prophecy the prophecy must remain obscure.

But that doesn't trouble the commentators. They blithely proceed to dogmatize about events to come; and they mistranslate the prophet to fit their wishful thinking. For instance, "an inundation" is interpreted as an invasion, "a bridge" becomes an alliance, and so on. There is seldom if ever any justification for these liberties.

S: Yes, I know they do such things. But don't you think, even when all allowance has been made for the faults of misinterpretation, that it is still possible to extract a variety of meanings from any one of the prophecies of Nostradamus? I remember reading once an article by the N. Y. Times book critic, Ralph Thompson, in which he said that if you stare at a prophecy of Nostradamus long enough, and go into a trance, you will be able to discover as many as fifteen meanings for it. As history repeats itself I think he's right.

I: That's pretty vague talk—vaguer than prophecy. History does repeat itself, but with innumberable differentiating details. Strictly speaking no two events are alike.

S: Yes, but does Nostradamus make that differentiation?

I: He does. You're a student of history, so let me fire at you some of his predictions. And I want you to try to interpret them of more than *one* historical situation.

S: That should not be hard.

I: Very well. One of the quatrains of the prophet begins, "In the year when a one-eyed man reigns in France . . ."

S: (*Surprised*) Does he actually say that?

I: He does.

S: Then I'm afraid you've got me there. I know that line can apply only to Henry the Second. He was pierced in the eye at a tournament.

I: Exactly. Which made him a one-eyed king. And he lived only a few days after the accident, so it was "in *the* year."

S: (*Not so sure of himself*) Ask me another.

I: "The Queen will be sent to death by jurors chosen by lot."

S: (*Suspiciously*) What's the French of that?

I: "La reine mise a mort, jurés a sort."

S: I'm afraid I'll have to give in again. I know of no queen in history outside of Marie Antoinette who was put to death by jurors chosen by lot.

I: When Nostradamus wrote that line there was not even a jury in France. The Revolutionists borrowed the idea from the English. But for the sake of argument let's assume that such an event did happen twice. Remember I have quoted only *one* line of the prophecy. The entire quatrain reads:

The government taken over will convict the King,
The Queen will be sent to death by jurors chosen by lot;
They will deny life to the Queen's son,

And the prostitute shares the fate of the consort.

All this happened at the time of that unique event when the queen was convicted by a jury. Her husband was guillotined, her son was put to death in the Temple, and Madame Du Barry, mistress of the preceding king, shared the fate of the queen. So you see that even if it had happened twice in history that a queen was put to death by jurors chosen by lot, the other contextual lines would restrict the meaning and make the prophecy inapplicable to any but the one situation. Besides, as there is no mention of any country in this prophecy France is meant.

S: Whew! Does Nostradamus actually say that?

I: Actually:

> Senat de Londres mettront â mort leur Roy.

When Nostradamus wrote, monarchs ruled by divine right. No king had ever been put to death by a parliament, whether in England or anywhere else. In his *Outline of History* Wells writes, "The English were drifting towards a situation new in the world's history, in which a monarch should be formally tried for treason to his people and condemned." Of the execution of Charles First he wrote, "This was indeed a great and terrifying thing that Parliament had done. The like of it had never been heard of in the world before." But Wells is wrong: One man had a scoop on it: Nostradamus.

S: Tell me, how many prophecies did he make like the ones you're giving me?

I: Here are a few more prophecies of events which were without precedent when Nostradamus, wrote, and which have only happened *once* since:

> More butcher than King in England,
> Born in an obscure place he will seize the Empire by force.
> His time approaches so near that I sigh.

S: Cromwell.

I: Yes, no one else. The rulers of England were naturally of royal birth. Cromwell was the exception. Besides, England did not begin to be an Empire till 1583, thirty years after this prophecy was penned. How about this one:

The great empire will be held by England,
The all-powerful, for more than three hundred years.

Again there is the mention of the Empire of England.
Not only was there no British Empire when Nostradamus
wrote these lines but England was only a minor European
power. Spain was the all-powerful nation.

S: I admit it is all very amazing, and that there are really a
multitude of his lines which cannot be applied to more than
one situation. How did he do it?

I: Prayer.

S: Is that all?

I: Isn't it enough?

S: I don't know: lots of people pray, but I've never heard of
them receiving information like that.

I: Then how would *you* explain it?

S: I can't. Perhaps your explanation is as good as any.

I: It's not merely mine: it's Nostradamus' own. Here are some
passages I culled from his introductory epistle to his son
Cesar, prefacing his book of prophecies:

"There is nothing that can be accomplished without Him,
whose power and goodness are so great to all His creatures
as long as they put their trust in Him, much as they may
be subject to other influences, yet on account of their likeness
to the nature of their good guardian angel, the heat and
prophetic power draws nigh to us, like the rays of the sun.
As for ourselves personally, who are but human, we can
attain to nothing by our own unaided natural knowledge,
nor the bent of our intelligence, in the way of deciphering
the recondite secrets of God the Creator. "It is not for you
to know the times or the seasons, which the Father hath put
in His own power. But ye shall receive power, after that the
Holy Ghost is come upon you."(Acts I:7,8)

"All things whatsoever proceed from the divine power
of the great eternal Deity from whom all goodness emanates.

"Further, my son, although I have inserted the name of
prophet, I do not desire to assume a title of so high sublimity
at the present moment. For, strictly speaking, my son, a
prophet is one who sees things remote from the knowledge
of all mankind. Or, to put the case: to the prophet, by means

of the perfect light of prophecy, there lie opened up very manifestly divine things as well as human; which cannot come about humanly, seeing that the effects of future prediction extend to such remote periods. Now, the secrets of God are incomprehensible, and their efficient virtue belongs to a sphere far remote from human knowledge; for, deriving their immediate origin from the free will, things set in motion causes that of themselves could never attract such attention as could make them recognized, either by human augury, or by any other knowledge of hidden power; it is a thing comprised only within the concavity of heaven itself, from the present fact of all eternity.

"The perfect knowledge of causes cannot be acquired without divine inspiration; since all prophetic inspiration derives its first motive principle from God the Creator, next from good fortune, and then from nature. For the human understanding, being intellectually created, cannot penetrate hidden causes, otherwise than by the thin flame of inspiration. The spirit of prophecy comes by an inpouring, which clarifies the supra- natural light, which is practically a participation in the divine eternity. Prophecy comes by knowing that what is predicted is true, and has had a heavenly origin; that such light and the thin flame is altogether efficacious; that it descends from above, no less than does natural light.

"The judgment perfects itself by means of the celestial judgment."

S: He must have been a very devout Christian.

I: He obviously believed God the only power, so naturally he turned to God for his inspiration.

S: Another thing that astonishes me is that his prophecies are so lucid. I had believed them vague.

I: Many of them are obscure—before the event. After the event they are clear. The error that Nostradamus wrote vaguely is spread unintentionally by casual commentators who approach the seer as they would a crystal-gazer. They are little interested in the prophecies already realized: but they are much interested in the prophecies still to be realized. So they attempt to "read" these quatrains hoping thereby to be able to interpret the future. The inquisitive reader knowing nothing about Nostradamus, picks up one of these current articles on the prophet and is straightway put into a profound puzzlement by a farrago of commentaries on predictions of events perhaps not to be realized for many years. No wonder he grows disgusted and puts down his paper or magazine with the exclamation, "You can interpret these prophecies any way you choose."

But what I quoted was clear to you. Besides, you are a student of history and that gave you the background for understanding the prognostications.

You heard eight of the prophecies. I could have quoted you eighty no less clear and unambiguous. Oddly enough perhaps, the verses of Nostradamus are much clearer than the verses of many of our poets who are not writing prophecy at all. Browning is obscure, John Donne is more so, but prophet Nostradamus is not. Even the emblems and symbols he employs in his writings are of the obvious kind. The Eagle is almost always Napoleon, the Cock is the French nation, and so on. And his anagrams are childishly simple.

S: Is he ever obscure?

I: Not often. Of course the prophecies not yet realized are for the most part obscure, but their obscurity lies simply in the fact that the event has not overtaken the prediction.

There are times when he is obscure with the obscurity of a scholar. You have studied Milton. You know that many of the English poet's passages are cloudy until the background is provided which enables one to interpret him. But his lines are not obscure in themselves: they are obscure only to the insufficiently equipped mind of the reader. So it is with Nostradamus, as learned a man as the English poet.

S: So what you telling me then is this: that when we do not understand Nostradamus it is either because he is writing of an event still to come, or because we lack the knowledge he possessed.

I: Exactly. Whenever we do find passages that to us seem obscure—and there are not so many of these—tackle them as we would difficult lines in Milton and they will clear up.

S: The lines you quoted to me were easy to understand.

I: Because Nostradamus is not one of the world's obscure writers.

Was Edgar Cayce Our American Nostradamus?

The answer to the above question is an emphatic no. but this sometimes genuine seer is too remarkable to be ignored. And one of his predictions in particular is too important to be left out of this book.

Here follows . . .

Edgar Cayce's Amazing Prophecy

Edgar Cayce (1876-1945), the trance sleeping-clairvoyant, seemed to be able to tune in on universal knowledge in his sleep, and come up with the correct answers to staggering problems more often than not. One set of his clairvoyant statements the author was personally interested in, made a special study of, and was able to follow through and check out. This concerned fluoridation, still an actively controversial subject. Cayce's trance judgments on the potent halogen are quoted in Jess Stearn's valuable book, *The Door To The Future*.

It was in September of 1943 that Cayce first considered the problem. This date makes his statements truly prophetic, for the fluoridation experiments were not carried out anywhere till 1945, the year of Cayce's death. In the late thirties and early forties the aluminum interests were confronted with a pressing problem. To produce aluminum they had to produce its deadly poisonous by- product, sodium fluoride. It was a real pollution problem, for no matter what container they used to hold the waste material, it was so corrosive it would eat through the metal, get into the ground and then into the ground waters.

When they dumped it into the rivers it killed the animals that drank there, and when they dumped it into the ocean, it killed the fish for miles around. The problem was not solved by putting the product in silos above the ground, for the fumes got to the vegetation, killed cattle and injured the farmers, and anyone else, who ate the polluted vegetables. The manufacturers had endless lawsuits and lost millions in damages. Soon they grew frantic. They couldn't put the stuff on the moon; they could sell only less than one per cent of it as rat poison, and it kept piling up.

Then a bright idea was conceived: An SOS was sent out to the press, offering a cash award for anyone who came up with a solution to the pollution problem. The award was won by Dr. Gerald Cox, researcher for the Alcoa-financed Mellon Institute. He had observed that in the areas in America where there was natural fluoride in the waters, the children apparently had fewer cavities. So he suggested, "Put the artificial fluoride in whatever public waters are fluoride-deficient and you will at the same time solve your pollution problem and improve the teeth of children everywhere."

No sooner said than done. Oscar Ewing, general counsel for Alcoa, was moved upstairs to the position of Under-Secretary of State, where he became the boss of 17 government agencies, including the U.S. Public Health Service. He promptly installed a fluoridation department and the disposal problem was solved.

All this took place in the last years of Cayce's life. It is not likely that he knew much about it, though the frantic clamor for help was in the newspapers. At any rate the fluoridation experiments were not begun till 1945, when Newburgh, New York and Grand Rapids, Michigan became the first experimental towns to be fluoridated. The results of these and other experiments were not known till years after Cayce's death.

A research dentist, however, who had heard something about the pending experiments, decided to question the "sleeping doctor," and it must be admitted that the statements he received from Cayce as far back as 1943 were remarkable. As Cayce reclined on his couch in a self-induced trance, the dentist asked:

"Is it true, as thought, that the intake of certain form and percentage of fluorine in drinking water causes mottled enamel of the teeth?"

The clairvoyant's answer may have seemed ambiguous, yet it was correct:

"This, to be sure, is true. But this is also untrue, unless there is considered the other properties with which such is associated in drinking water."

It is now well known to those who have investigated the effect of fluoridation on children's teeth that mottling is caused. "Damaging mottling" has been reported in the famous British medical magazine, *The Lancet,* and severe mottling in New Mexico, Sheboygan, Wisconsin and many other areas. Yet on February 27, 1967, Dr. Ast, head of the USPHS at Albany, countering reports from Grand Rapids of 20% damaging mottling of the teeth of white children and 40% of those of Negro children, gave proof of no mottling whatever of teeth of Negro children under fluoridation elsewhere. As Cayce observed, *other factors* must be considered along with the fluoridation. So his answer "yes and no" is quite correct.

Cayce went on in sleep: "If there are certain percents of fluoride with free limestone, we will find it beneficial."

This is a remarkable statement. Fluorine's first love is for calcium, and where there is calcium in the water it combines with it, forming calcium fluoride. Of recent date many medical men are now suspicious that it is the *calcium* in the calcium fluoride and not the *fluoride* in the calcium fluoride that does the trick. Besides, this natural fluoride is found in hard waters containing magnesium and other elements helpful to teeth.

And then it would seem that in his next statement Cayce's psychic power partly failed him:

"If there are certain percents with indications of magnesium, sulfur and the like, we will have, one, mottling; another, decaying at the gum."

It is believed today by scientists that fluoride does its greatest harm in soft waters, not in hard, which contains magnesium and other helpful buffers. However, even here, some of Cayce's clairvoyant ability shone through. He was not only aware of the harmful mottling, now reluctantly admitted by our fluoridationists, but quite correct about tooth decay: five years after fluoridation in Miami the children's teeth had gone so bad that the matter became the subject of horrified headlines and articles in the *The Miami Herald.* And Dr. H. K. Box, a periodontist of international repute on the Dental Faculty of the University of Toronto, has found "appalling periodontal disease" in areas where the water has been fluoridated.

Cayce's next statements seem off the track. He warned: "Where there is iron or sulfur or magnesium, be careful!" But it would be interesting if the future proves him to have been correct here also!

The sleeping seer went on to indicate the need for tests prior to fluoridating the water supplies. And then came a truly astonishing statement: that fluoridation would be harmful "in such a district as Illinois.".

Thereby hangs a tale. Studies published by the University of Wisconsin in 1956 showed a higher incidence of mongoloid children born in areas where the water was fluoridated than where it was not. Also, there were indications that there is a cause-effect relationship between the amount of fluoride in the water supply and the number of mongoloid children born.

This evidence was not appealing to those who advocated adding fluoride to public water supplies; but it took them two years to catch their breath. Then they were able to applaud a report by Dr. W.T.C. Berry, of the British Ministry of Health, who stated that investigation of naturally fluoridated waters in England showed no such correlation between mongolism and fluoridation. Although he did not claim his results statistically significant, the fluoridationists were now able to jeer at the University of Wisconsin "scare" report. A prominent fluoridationist, Dr. A. L. Russell suggested that the ideal place for "a proper study" would be Illinois, where the fluoride tables, under Dr. Elvove and Dr. Russell's confrere, were so accurate; he said it was a big state and would give "an accurate sampling." Such a study, he said, "would be rather simple and quite accurate." Dr. Rapaport accepted the challenge. He engaged the cooperation of five pro-fluoridationists, including Mr. Bridger, chief statistician of the State of Illinois Department of Public Health. The figures for Illinois on mongolism were supplied by the Department of Health and the data were impersonally processed with IBM equipment. The results were scandalous. Whereas, in the first University of Wisconsin study, the probability was fifty to one that fluoride causes mongolism, the more perfect Illinois study, carried out according to the advice of Dr. Russell, gave a probability of 1000 to 1 that fluoride causes mongolism.

Dr. Rapaport's reports are now published in reputable French medical journals, but no longer in The United States!

So Cayce's prediction that fluoridation in Illinois would prove harmful has been amply borne out. Indeed, Illinois is the one and only state in the Union where such a study has been carried out so completely.

Coming Events Cast Their Shadows

Edgar Cayce was by no means an infallible prophet, but he was so often astonishingly correct. Take, for instance, his prediction concerning Norfolk Harbor, made August 27th, 1932: within thirty years it would become the chief port on the East Coast, "this not excepting Philadelphia or New York." According to the pamphlet *Earth Changes* Published by the ARE Press, Norfolk Harbor and the Port of Newport News together shipped and imported "a total of 59,920 tons of cargo." Ports of the Delaware River and tributaries were second, and New York Harbor third.

Cayce's predictions regarding the destruction of California have caused a good deal of consternation. Jess Stearn's book on the Sleeping Psychic devotes an entire chapter to the subject.

In an article entitled *The Future,* by "Jan Van Goh," who writes for *Fate* and *Exploring the Unknown* under his real name of Curtis Gibson, was predicted: in the 1970's or 80's a strip of California's coast, from near Long Beach to about 1,000 miles north of Los Angeles, averaging 10 or 15 miles wide, will suddenly sink beneath the Pacific, in our country's greatest natural disaster *up till then* (except perhaps the first Great American Famine).

New York City may suffer both natural and A-bomb destructions near the end of the century.

According to Edgar Cayce, destruction of New York will take place no later than 1998. Jim Gavin, the irish true-dreamer who has had some fantastic hits, believes New York's time of trouble is very near. He sees Staten Island sinking like a raft being pulled under water, and Manhattan Island also sinking from its lower tip up to 59th Street.

Curtis Gibson also predicts:

Great increase in weather violence and severity, and especially of gold, with the whole North Atlantic freezing over for months at a time, and snow reaching a depth of 30 feet (on a level) in U.S. and 60 feet in Russia. Many freakish cloudbursts and earthquakes, and temporary coastal inundations due to local superphysical interference with nature.

Between 2010 and 2020 will come the greatest natural disaster of all: a sudden shift of the Earth's axis of some 30 degrees will send mile high waves of the Atlantic ocean water rolling across the U.S. Atlantic coastal plain.

One of the first disastrous land sinkings will leave most of Sicily beneath the sea, as it will tilt southward.

Our southeastern coastline will be greatly extended, and our South California coast much less. Later a land bridge will rise from Scotland to North America, and part of Mu, about the size and shape of Greenland or Madagascar, will emerge 1000 miles West of Mexico.

The great peak of the Amne Machin, in West China, will be found to be the world's highest, at least 31,000 feet, and will be named Conton Peak...

The 49 year Time of Jacob's Trouble, the Night of Antichrist, is also the Golden Age, hence a paradox and mystery. It is the smelting pot in which the heat of human strife and cruelty, joined with equally severe natural disasters and cruel punishment, will melt and separate the dross of human folly and vanity and the gold of our divine potential, and the latter will sink completely out of sight for a time so that evil seems to be wholly the victor, but at Armageddon, the Judgment of the Nations Jove Goldsmith will open the slag-drain; the slag-folk will pour into the bottomless pit; 'then shall the Righteous, the golden, shine in their glory,' through the long Millennium Sabbath of rest and peace, reign of Lord Sabaoth, Prince of Peace.

Cayce's predictions for approximately the same periods are in some respects similar. Summarized, he says:

The greater portion of Japan must go into the sea (contradicted by Curtis Gibson).

The upper portion of Europe will be changed as in the twinkling of an eye.

Land will appear off the east coast of America.

There will be upheavals in the Arctic and in the Antarctic that will make for the eruption of volcanoes in the torrid areas, and there will be the shifting then of the poles—so that where there have been those frigid or semi-tropical, will become the more tropical, and moss and fern will grow.

None of these predictions do I present dogmatically.

Two strange troubles, so far unfulfilled, may also belong to this era. I am inclined to think they are not nature's, but man- made; a Nostradamus quatrain reads:

great horror will come out of Lausanne,
So that one will not know the origin of the deed.
One will put out all the people from afar,
Fire seen in the heavens, foreign people undone.

(8.10)

Nostradamus almost invariably uses the term foreign, or *étrange,* for the Germans. The horror may be an explosion. Whatever it is, its destruction is so thorough that it leaves no trace of its origin.

Is it possible that the next quatrain refers to a dangerous breakdown of an atomic reactor?

Migrate, migrate from Geneva everyone of you,
Saturn of gold will change to iron,
The counter RAYPOZ will exterminate all,
Before the event there will be signs in the sky.

(9.44)

Plans have already been laid to set up an atomic reactor in Geneva, Switzerland, but as safely as possible: by building underground. Sweden has similar plans.

Nevertheless, the reactor is not safe. The Atomic Energy Commission has reported that a single accident to a major nuclear plant could cost 3,400 lives, injure some 43,000 people, and cause property damage of seven billion dollars.

A scientist writing from Switzerland poses this problem: Krypton 90 is a gaseous by-product of nuclear plants. It is vented into the atmosphere, as it can not be trapped by filters in the sacks. Its short half-life of two seconds accomplishes its decay into Rubidium 90, which in some minutes becomes Strontium 90. This last is dangerously radio-active, with a half- life of 28 years.

Long-lived radio-active fallout would make it under stand-able why all the people should not merely leave, but — as

Nostradamus writes — *migrate*.

A Prophecy On the Russian Revolution

A quatrain of Nostradamus on the Russian Revolution is so clear as to need no interpretation:

Songs, chants and slogans of the Slavic people
While princes and Lord are captive in the prisons,
In the future, by idiots without heads
Will be received as divine oracles.

(1.14)

What is worthy of note, however, is that Nostradamus, who devotes so many prophecies to the French Revolution, considers the Russian Revolution of much less importance, for scarcely any of his quatrains concern the Soviet New Order. Also, his attitudes towards the two revolutions are contrasts. In describing the French Revolution his feelings evince harrowed horror, but towards the Russian Revolution and its fruits he feels only scorn.

The paucity of Nostradamus prophecies on Communism would indicate that the Soviet land is not, for too long, to be "a troubler of the poor world's peace."

And signs that Russia's communistic empire is breaking down are becoming evident to the world. Columnist Richard Reeves (August 1984) cites significant squabbling between the USSR and East Germany, signalizing the beginning of a breakup of the Soviet Eastern-European Empire. East and West Germany may reunite. The satellites are restless. "Poland is in sullen revolt." Romania has gone to the Los Angeles Olympics. Hungary has shown our Olympics on TV.

The following quatrain concerns the failure of Communism:

The law of More will be seen to decline:

After another much more seductive:
Boristhenes first will come to fail:
Through the gifts and tongue of another more attractive.

(3.95)

Sir Thomas More's *Utopia* concerned a communistic commonwealth. This celebrated idealistic fiction was published in Latin in 1516, during Nostradamus' school days. "The law of More" would be understood by any of the prophet's contemporaries as a reference to Communism. The Boristhenes is the Dnieper. Edgar Leoni comments:

> For the reader in the second half of the 20th century, this is one of the most interesting of all the prophecies of Nostradamus—one full of portentous meaning for this era, after having had none from the 16th to the 20th centuries. We now have the generic name 'communism' to apply to the utopian ideologies of which Sir Thomas More's *Utopia* is the common ancestor. ... The prophecy implies a widespread success of this ideology prior to its decline, and mentions that the decline will start where the Dnieper is located. This is the principal river of the Ukraine. In Nostradamus' day it was one of the most backward parts of Europe, part of the Polish-Lithuanian state for three hundred years, and hardly an area Nostradamus would choose for the locale involving any contemporary movement of this nature, such as the Anabaptists. Accordingly, it is not unreasonable to speculate on a possible 20th century fulfillment of this prophecy, involving the Soviet Ukraine and perhaps its chief city (which is on the Dnieper), Kiev. The nature of the more seductive law and more attractive tongue are subjects for further speculation.

The paucity of prophecies of Nostradamus on Communism was negative evidence which enabled the author for years, on radio and on lecture platforms, to state categorically that there would be no war between the United States and Russia. His reasoning was that if there were going to be a war between these two giants it would be a World War and Nostradamus would have had many quatrains about it. Even in the thick of the Cuban crisis, discussing Nostradamus; prophecies on the Long John radio show, the author stated flatly that Castro would not involve us in war with the communist world.

With Russian Communism a failure, the author asks, what

will replace it? Apparently something positive. Oscar Wilde predicted: "The White Christ will come out of Russia," and Edgar Cayce predicted similarly:

> Through Russia comes the hope of the world. Not in respect to what is sometimes termed Communism or Bolshevism. No. But freedom, freedom! That each man will live for his fellow man. The principle has been born there. It will take years for it to be crystallized. Yet out of Russia comes the hope of the world.

Jess Stearn, in his book on Edgar Cayce, comments: "As many have begun to suggest plausibly, in view of the growing peril to the West from China, he saw Russia eventually merging in friendship with the United States. 'By what will Russia be guided? By friendship with that nation which hath even placed on its monetary unit *In God We Trust.*'"

Again Cayce said: "On Russia's religious development will come the greater hope of the world. Then that one, or group, that is the closer in its relationship, may fare better in gradual changes and final settlement of conditions as to the rule of the world."

In Armageddon time, it is possible that a part of Russia may be against the forces of light, but if so, it will be unwillingly. In the Bible, Gog and Magog—generally interpreted as Russia—will have "hooks in its jaws" and will be forced to fight for the Arab Antichrist; but a great deal of Russia, deeply Christian by then, will be with us in spirit and body.

The Bible Tells Our Destiny

The Americans, British and Celts are the real "chosen people," according to Biblical interpreters. These are held to be the lost tribes of Israel, which shall be reunited.

Quoth a Nazi: *"Roosevelt is a Jew! Translate his name from Dutch into German and you get Rosenfeld. Besides, he had a great-grandfather named Isaac."*

Such and similar cant has frequently been heard among our Bundists and Coughlinites. Why? Do they not know that one of the biggest chiefs of Naziland is named Rosenberg—and that name does not need translation from the Dutch, either. Surely then if the Germans can have a mountain of roses Americans may have a field of them. And as for the Hebrew name the cultured Nazis never heard of ABRAHAM Lincoln, ISAAC Newton, and JACOB Astor? Do these names make their possessors Jews? No. We anglo-Saxons study the Bible, and we often take our names from the Bible.

On the other hand, it is undeniable that Roosevelt *is* an Israelite. And so am I, reader, and so are you. And the same goes for all who are of the Anglo-Saxon-Celtic race. Even Coughlin, Nye, Pelley, Lindbergh, and all our Christian Fronters are Israelites, and there is nothing they can do about it.

We are Israelites, but not necessarily Jews. Every Jew is an Israelite, but every Israelite is not a Jew, just as every Scotsman is a Britisher, but every Britisher is not a Scotsman.

This briefly is the story: according to the Bible the Israelites were once one house, and were collectively called Israel. But with the death of King Solomon the Northern Ten Tribes revolted and set up a separate kingdom, known as the Kingdom of Israel. Taxes caused the split. The two southern tribes, Judah and Benjamin, became known as the Kingdom of Judah. Judah (or Yehudah) has survived. "Jew" is an abbreviation of this name. But apparently ten-tribed Israel was lost to history when in the eighth century B.C. it was carried into captivity by the warlike Assyrians. Yet Bible prophecy insists that the two kingdoms will be restored and united in the last days. The Jewish Chronicle states, "The Scriptures speak of a future restoration of Israel, which is clearly to include both Judah and Ephraim. The problem, then is reduced to its simplest form. The ten tribes are certainly in existence. All that has to be done is to discover which people represent them."

We now have overwhelming evidence as to "which people represent them." Ten-tribed Israel migrated to the British Isles over a period of centuries, and Israel is today revealed as the Anglo-Saxon-Celtic race.

Differences In Resemblance

"But if the Jews are our brothers, why do we not all look alike?" The answers are several: in the first place Judah and Israel have been separated nationally for over two thousand five hundred years. In that time physiognomies can change a good deal. Remember too that the twelve sons of Israel were by different mothers. Leah and Rachel, though sisters, were very unlike each other. Joseph was not recognized by his brothers, nor even known to be a Hebrew. Paul was mistaken for an Egyptian (Acts 21:38).

Geography makes a difference. James Bryce, F.R.S., gives an example of its effect upon racial features: "Without any intermingling of red and white men, the modern American, thanks to climatic conditions, resembles the Red Indian far more closely than he does his own ancestors of the Colonial days."

The children of the captivity were often painted by the ancient Egyptians. Professor Sayce states that these works of art were executed with "photographic fidelity." On the walls of the temple of Karnak, portraits in bas relief of the Israelites reveal "a fair-haired, blue-eyed, dolichocephalic race much resembling those of the present Nordic North." Sir J. Gardner Wilkinson, in his *Ancient Egypt*, writes, "I may mention a remarkable circumstance, that the Jews of the East to this day often have red hair and blue eyes, with a nose of delicate form and nearly straight, and are quite unlike their brethren of Europe." (It is interesting to note here that Tom Ireland in his *History of Ireland*, relates, "A branch of the ancient Celts called Gael— generally tall, *reddish-fair- haired and blue-eyed*—started the conquest of Ireland three or four centuries before Christ.".)

The Blond Jews

A few years ago in Rumania a German official was nearly mobbed by antiSemites because he had fair hair. William B. Ziff, authority on Palestine, tells me that he stood on a street corner in Tel-Aviv, counted the heads of Jewish boys and found that nine out of ten were fair-haired. Spanish Jews are fair-haired in the midst of a dark-haired people. Halevy, the great Jewish poet, praising the beauty of his beloved, gloried in her golden tresses.

The positive evidence as to our Hebrew origin is even more startling. No less an authority than the great Orientalist and "Father of Assyriology," Sir Henry Rawlinson, wrote, after deciphering the trilingual inscriptions on the Behistun Rock: "The ethnic name Gimri occurs in the cuneiform writing of the time of Darius. It is the equivalent of the Greek Cimmeri, and of the Danish Cymbri, and of the Welsh Khumri. *We have reasonable grounds for regarding the Gimri, or Cimmerians, . . . and the Sacae of the Behistun Rock . . . as identical with Israel.*"

Now, it is a well known historical fact that the Sacae (who were Scythians of whom Herodotus said, "They eat no pork, nor keep swine for profit") were the Saxons. It is also an undisputed fact that the Welsh are Khumri: they call themselves so still.

The English scholar Adam Rutherford (not the late Judge) writes, "The relationship between Hebrew and Welsh is so close that it would be difficult to adduce a single article or form of construction in the Hebrew Grammar, but the same is to be found in Welsh, and there are many whole sentences in both languages exactly the same in the very words." Dr. Davies, the author of a Welsh Grammar book, says that "almost every page of the Welsh translation of the Bible is replete with Hebraisms in the time, sense, and spirit of the original."

Similarly there are thousands of words in Irish that are of Hebrew origin. For instance, O'Hart says that the ancient capital of Ireland, Tara, took its name from the Hebrew word Torah, or law. And Thomas Moore, Irish historian, writes with puzzlement, "It is remarkable that all the ancient altars found in Ireland and now distinguished by the name of Cromleck, or sloping stones, were originally called Bothal, the House of God, and they seem to be of the same species as those mentioned in the book of Genesis and called by the Hebrews Bethel, which has the same significance as the Irish Bothal."

The religion of the Irish and the Welsh was known as Druidism. Cassell's *History of England* states, "The Druidical rites and ceremonies were almost identical with the Mosaic ritual." Charles Hulbert, in his *Religions of Britain,* writes, "So near is the resemblance between the Druidical religion of Britain and the Patriarchal religion of the Hebrews, that we hesitate not to pronounce their origin the same."

Two Popular Fallacies

1. That The British Are A Mongrel Race:

No doubt certain Irishmen will feel surprised at this, and at the following remarks by Sir Arthur Keith, one of the world's greatest scientists: "Except for a trick of speech or local mannerism, the most expert anthropologist cannot tell a Celt from a Saxon, or an Irishman from a Scotsman . . . From the physical point of view the Celt and Saxon are one; whatever be the source of their mutual antagonism, it does not lie in a difference of race. It is often said that we British are a mixed and mongrel collection of types and breeds; the truth is, that as regards physical type the inhabitants of the British Isles are the most uniform of all the large nationalities of Europe."

2. That The British Druids Offered Human Sacrifices:

This view has been promulgated even in some British school- books, But historian Charles Hulbert states in his *Religions of Britain;* "The charge of staining their consecrated places with human blood and offering, upon the altar of Stonehenge, human victims, has no real foundation in fact; an accusation as wicked as unjust." Dr. Kinnamon, noted American archaeologist, writes, "Dr. Petrie had the temerity to lift the great altar at Stonehenge, and found beneath it only the burnt bones of cattle." So little cruelty was there in the nature of the Druids, that, unlike the Romans, they would not even imprison their debtors!

Anglo-Saxons Are Among The "Chosen" People

In an Anglo-Israel pamphlet entitled "The Pattern of History," there is this challenge: "Let us see which nation or race now fulfills God's promises regarding the future of Israel. There are many such Promises. We shall give eight of them here to show what they indicate:

1. Israel is to be a Powerful Nation. (Micah 4:7; 5:8)
2. Israel would be living Northwest of Palestine. (Jer. 31:8; 23:8; 3:18; Isa. 24:15).
3. Israel is to be mistress of the Ends, Sides, and Uttermost Parts of the Earth. (Deut. 33:17; Ps. 98:3; 2:8).
4. Israel is to hold a Great Heathen Empire in Dominion. (Isa. 54:3).
5. Israel is to be the Chief Missionary Power of the Earth, carrying the Gospel everywhere. (Isa. 49:6; 27:6; Micah 5:7).
6. Israel is to become a Nation and a Company of Nations. (Gen. 35:11).
7. Israel is to be Immune from Defeat in War. (Isa. 17:14; 41:12,15; 54:17).
8. Part of Israel is to have split off from the Mother Country and have become a great people in their own right. (Isa. 49:19,20).
9. Possessing the Gates of their Enemies (Gen. 22:17).
10. An Island or Coast People (Isa. 24:15; 41:1; Jer. 31:10).
11. The Chief Nations (Isa. 41:8,9).
12. With Colonies in all zones, immense in size (Isa. 54:1-3; 58:12; Obad. 17).
13. Scattered everywhere among the Heathen (Ezek. 37:21).
14. With Possessions forming a great girdle round the Gentile Nations (Deut. 32:7,9).
15. Immensely wealthy (Deut. 28:1-14; Isa. 60:16; Jer. 31:12).

16. Lending to all Nations — borrowing from none (Deut. 28:1-14).
17. Abiding always by their ancient Israelitish, perfectly just and God-given system of weights and measures (Lev. 19:36).
18. Kind as a rule to the aborigines of their Colonies, but finding them, to their distress, "Dying out" before them (Jer. 30:10-11).
19. A Christian Nation — redeemed from the curse of the Law (Isa. 45:17; 48:20).
20. A Sabbath keeping Race, Nationally and by Law (Ezek. 31:17).
21. Yet alas! prone to Idolatry and ever lapsing into it (Hos. 8:11).
22. Addicted, as regards very many of the people to all sorts of wickedness and abominations, hateful to God (Ezek, 37:23).
23. Nationally addicted to the vice of drunkenness (Isa. 28).
24. Blind as to their Origin (Hosea 2:6).
25. Ever declaring they are not God's People Israel (Hosea 1:10).
26. Two Great Rival Nations were to spring from Joseph (Gen. 48:13,20).
27. The Lord undertakes to fight against all who fight against Israel (Isa. 41:8-14; 49:25, 26; 52:12; 54:15, 17).
28. Israel is to be kind to the poor (Deut. 15:7-11).
29. Israel is to have dominion from sea to sea (Ps. 72:8).
30. Israel is to be gentle and magnanimous in victory (1 Kings 20:31).
31. Israel is to be kind to the aliens in their land (Lev. 19:33).
32. To again possess Palestine (Jer. 31:5).
33. A multitudinous people previous to repossessing Palestine (Hos. 1:10).
34. Israel's gathering to be in the West (Isa. 43:5).

"These eight identifying marks are really enough in themselves to show who present-day Israel must be. Remember, all these marks must apply to Israel today.

"How many great nations living northwest of Palestine have never known defeat in war? There are only two—the United

States and the British Commonwealth of Nations—*the nations which are considered Anglo-Saxon.* A civil war, of course, cannot be considered war in the sense that it is used here; naturally, when one part of Israel fights another, one or the other must be defeated. The United States has never lost a war. Britain has lost only to the United States. Even in the dim periods of history, the only nations which defeated Britain were themselves of Israel descent—such as the Normans.

"One *race*, and one race alone, has all these marks. Nations within this race may have only a portion of them, but the race *as a whole* has them all. That race is *the Anglo- Saxon-Celtic peoples.*"

Israel In The Isles

In the following passages from the book of Isaiah the prophet is *addressing Israel*, and *after* they have become a lost people:

"Listen, O Isles, unto me." (49:1)
"Keep silence before me, O Islands." (41:1)
"To the Islands he will repay recompense." (59:18)
"The Isles shall wait for His law." (42:4)
"Sing unto the Lord a new song, and his praise from the end of the earth, ye that go down to the sea, and all that is therein; the isles, and the inhabitants thereof." (42:10)
"Let them give glory unto the Lord, and declare his praise in the Islands." (42:12)

Moffat translates "Islands" as "coastlands," which of course islands are too — but the consensus of scholarly opinion, including that of the Revised Version — is for "islands." That such is the meaning intended is obvious from Isaish 40:15, "Behold, He taketh up the isles as a very little thing." Other references to "isles" in the Bible tell us that they were north and west of Palestine.

What Isles?

Long before the Anglo-Israel theory was ever promulgated it was known that the isles referred to were the British. As far back as the year 1220, the learned Rabbi David Kimchi wrote, "The 'islands of the sea' of Isaiah II, belonged (in the past) to the Roman Empire." In the first quarter of the 18th century, Dr. Abbadie of Amsterdam, after a careful study of the Bible references to Israel in the Isles, wrote, "unless the ten tribes have flown in the air, or have been plunged to the centre of the earth, they must be sought for in the North and West, and in the British Isles." The Reverend M. S. Bergmann, who translated the Bible into Yiddish, wrote: "I have no hesitation in saying that Great Britain is meant by 'the isles afar off' mentioned by the prophets. This has been the opinion of many ancient and modern Jewish theologians. The late Rev. Dr. Margoliouth held, in common with many other Hebrews, that these 'isles' were supposed to have been Britannia, Scotia, and Hibernia."

The Word of the Lord to Israel in the Isles

Keep silence before me, O Islands; and let the people renew their strength... Thou, Israel, art my servant, Jacob whom I have chosen, the seed of Abraham my friend. Fear thou not; for I am with thee: be not dismayed; for I am thy God: I will strengthen thee; yea, I will help thee; yea, I will uphold thee with the right hand of my righteousness behold, all they that were incensed against thee shall be ashamed and confounded: *they shall be as nothing; and they that strive with thee shall perish. Thou shalt seek them, and shalt not find them, even them that contended with thee:* They that war against thee shall be as nothing, and as a thing of naught.

The British Are Not Germanic

The shape of the head is now held to be one of the best available tests of race known... The most remarkable trait of the population of the British Isles is in the head form, and especially the uniformity in this respect which is everywhere manifested... The facts indicate a remarkable invariability of cranial type compared with the results obtained elsewhere... Thus the ethnological comparison proves that the Anglo-Saxon peoples must be of an entirely different stock from the present German race, and that they, therefore, do not belong to the Teuton stock.

Prof. W. J. Ripley, *in The Races of Europe.*

The High Aryanization of Britain, and the relatively low Aryanization of Germany with its round-heads, may in part explain the desire of Caesar to incorporate Britain, and his determination to exclude Germany from incorporation, in the

Roman Empire. (Lines written in 1923)
Colonel Waddell, contributor to *Encyclopedia Britannica*.

The Meaning of "Chosen People"

God is no respecter of persons. All who do His will are true Israelites. And His gifts are distributed among all peoples. The Germans were "chosen" for music, the Dutch for painting, etc., etc. Israel was chosen for service, not for superiority. She was chosen to inhabit the waste places of the earth and to spread the ideals of Scriptural democracy everywhere. The Stone Kingdom must cover the earth.

Are foreigners who come here to live Israelites? Yes, we assimilate them all. Say a boy is born over here of Italian parents. He is subject to their influence. But he goes to an American school and is taught American ideals, American history, and American and English literature. He mingles with American boys and plays American games. He reads American newspapers, Americans funnies. He goes to American movies which fill his mind with American romantic aspirations. American influence presses upon him continuously from all sides. Result: he becomes a true Israelite.

The Key To Bible Prophecy

Without an understanding of Anglo-Israelism it is impossible to understand any but a few of the prophecies of the Bible. But with this key the prophetic Scriptures become an open book, and our destiny is revealed. We are the people for whom these prophecies were made. This does not mean that the Bible was not written for all men: its spiritual teachings are for mankind: but the prophecies are for Israel and Judah.

With this understanding that we are Israel, our national duty as well as destiny becomes clearer. We are the "chosen" people, chosen not for *superiority* but for *service*.

And now, saith the Lord that formed me from the womb to be his servant, to bring Jacob again to him, Though Israel be not gathered, yet shall I be glorious in the eyes of the Lord, and my God shall be my strength. And he said, It is a light thing that thou shouldest be my servant to raise up the tribes of Jacob, and to restore the preserved of Israel: *I will also give thee for a light to the gentiles, that thou mayest be my salvation unto the end of the earth.* (Isa. 49:5,6.)

We must bring the Four Freedoms to the entire world, even "unto the end of the earth." This will be a mighty task, but an inescapable one. Britain and America are daily gravitating nearer and nearer to each other. The result will be federation, and inevitably all power will pass to the Anglo-Saxon-Celtic peoples. Then we will be *forced* into the position of world's policeman, and our guide-book must then be the Holy Bible if we are not to act ruinously.

According to Bible prophecy, Americans, British, and Jews are to have One Flag. The prophecies of the Bible iterate and re- iterate that *all* Israel is to be reunited in the latter days. The most famous of these prophecies is that of Ezekiel, with its weird and striking imagery:

Tongues of Israelite Origin

The striking similarity between the Hebrew and the Welsh and Irish languages is cited as one proof that the Celtic peoples came from Israel. Here are examples:

ENGLISH	HEBREW	IRISH
father	Ab	Ab
war-cry	Aboi	Abu
shoemaker	Asar	Asaire
woman,light	Bahin	Ban
son	Bar	Bar
desire, strength	Chail	Cail
old woman	Calach	Cailliac
society	Sanhedrim	Saindrean
granary	Schibol	Sciobal
this	So	So
heaven, brightness	Zion	Sion

Thousands of similar examples can be found. In the following table the same similarity is evident in Hebrew and Welsh.

95

ENGLISH	WELSH	HEBREW
Job answered, O	Yngan Job yscoli	Jangan Iub ascol
that my grief were	yscoli cynghawsi	iascel
thoroughly weighed	cangesi	
Thy terrors have		
cut me off	Angheni a gowan	Angini eu gouan
Thou hast healed me	Iachaddni	Ichiiathni
Madness and		
blindness	Ysgoefon a gwirion	Isgoahvon u giwaeon
Rain, etc.	Gaenen oer fo	Gaenan Ourvo
None did compel	An annos	Aen aones
An angry man	As chwimwth	Aischemouth

(From A. A. Ackley's *From Abraham to America*)

The Valley Of The Bones

The hand of the Lord was upon me, and carried me out in the spirit of the Lord, and set me down in the midst of the valley which was full of bones. And caused me to pass by them round about: and, behold, there were very many in the open valley; and lo, they were very dry. And he said unto me, Son of man, can these bones live? And I answered, O Lord God, thou knowest. Again he said unto me, Prophesy upon these bones, and say unto them, O ye dry bones, hear the word of the Lord. Thus saith the Lord God unto these bones; Behold, I will cause breath to enter into you, and ye shall live: And I will lay sinews upon you, and will bring up flesh upon you, and cover you with skin, and put breath in you, and ye shall live; and ye shall know that I am the Lord.

So I prophesied as I was commanded: and as I prophesied, there was a noise, and behold a shaking, and the bones came together, bone to his bone. And when I beheld, lo, the sinews and the flesh came up upon them, and the skin covered them above: but there was no breath in them.

Then said He unto me, Prophesy unto the wind... Thus saith the Lord God; Come from the four winds, O breath, and breathe upon these slain, that they may live. So I prophesied as he commanded me, and the breath came into them, and they lived, and stood up upon their feet, an exceeding great army.

Then He said unto me, Son of man, these bones are the whole house of Israel: behold, they say, Our bones are dried, and our hope is lost: we are cut off our parts. Therefore prophesy and say unto them, Thus saith the Lord God: Behold, O my people, I will open your graves, and cause you to come up out of your graves, and bring you into the land of Israel. And ye shall know that I am the Lord... And I shall put my spirit in you, and ye shall live, and I shall place you in your own land: then shall ye know that I the Lord have spoken it, and performed it, said the Lord.

The word of the Lord came again unto me, saying, Moreover, thou son of man, take thee one stick, and write upon it, For Judah, and for the children of Israel his companions: then take another stick, and write upon it, For Joseph, the stick of Ephraim, and for all the house of Israel his companions. And join them one to another into one stick; and they shall become one in thine hand ...And I will make them one nation in the land upon the mountains of Israel; and *one king shall be king to them all: and they shall be no more two nations, neither shall they be divided into two kingdoms any more at all*

(Ezek.37).

That Britain and America shall be re-united under one flag is understood by millions who are unaware that both the Bible and Nostradamus predicted it. But how about the Jews, scattered among the many nations of the earth?

Zionist Success Prophesied

The answer is to be found in the Jewish recolonization of Palestine. One Bible prophecy about it is in the process of fulfillment:

In those days, the House of Judah shall walk to the House of Israel. (The "to" is in the marginal note of the Revised Version) and they shall come together out of the land of the north, to the land that I have given for an inheritance unto your fathers (Jer. 3:18).

Our Lord prophesied that "Jerusalem shall be trodden down of the Gentiles until the Times of the Gentiles be fulfilled" (Luke 21:24). It was in December, 1917, that Allenby walked bareheaded into Jerusalem, which he had wrested from the Turk. Palestine was again in the hand of Israel. In November, 1917, the House of Judah walked to the House of Israel when the Zionist Confederation successfully petitioned the British

Government to reopen the Holy Land to Jewish immigration.

At present there are about a half-million Jews in Palestine. So the prophecy is by no means fulfilled. Nor are the British and Americans yet under the one flag. But the signs of near fulfillment are very evident. In these latter days, prophesies Isaiah, "the desert shall bloom like the rose." This is now Happening with the immigration of the Jews to the Holy Land.

The well-known English writer, Beverly Nichols, remarks:

> As I walked around, I became more and more astonished that any race of men, let alone intellectual Jews, could possibly tackle such an unfriendly soil... Yet over this wilderness the exclerks, ex-doctors, ex-clerks swarmed like ants, staggering under the weight of the stones they were removing, panting as they wielded their spades.

The fulfillment of Isaiah's prophecy is on the way. And it will be fulfilled completely in the course of the century.

"But," some will say, "is it not prophesied that the *whole* House of Israel is to be restored to Palestine? And how can all Americans and the British move into the Holy Land? We do not want to do that, and we could not if we did want to." Bible prophecy, however, is to be fulfilled, and correctly fulfilled. Jeremiah prophesies of Israel: "I will take you one of a city and two of a family and I will bring you to Zion." The Anglo-Saxons will be established in the Holy Land by reparesentation; but to the Jews, Jerusalem will be their homeland.

But this goal may not be realized without conflict with the Arabs. Which brings us logically and naturally into the next chapter.

SYMBOLS OF ISRAEL

The great seal of Manasseh reproduced on our dollar bills Since 1935!

According to the Bible, Reuben, one of the 12 children of Jacob(Isrtael) did evil in the sight of the Lord. Hence he lost the birthright to the two sons of Joseph: Ephraim and Manasseh. The second of these sons prophetically represents America, since it was Manasseh who broke away from Ephraim(Israel) and became a great and independent Israelitish nation. Manasseh was tribe number thirteen, and that number is represented on the Great Seal, since America consisted of thirteen states when it broke away from the Mother Country.

The Great Seal of America and the Great Crest of England are emblematic of the origin of Manasseh and Ephraim, the children of Joseph by an Egyptian wife. The two most famous monuments of Egypt are the universally recognized Sphinx and Pyramid. Our Great Seal has the Pyramid; one of Britain's insignia has the Sphinx. The next most famous monument of Egypt is the obelisk. There were three of these standing in sight of the Temple of On when the children of Joseph played there thousands of years ago. One of the obelisks remains in Egypt. Of the remaining two, one is in London, the other in New York.

The British Coat of Arms consists of *four* Israelitish emblems: the Lion and the Unicorn (emblems of Ephraim mentioned with Balaam's blessing), the harp of David, and the inscription, which translated reads: "My God and my Right" (Ephraim's birthright).

The Irish And The Jews

The Irish are brothers of the Jews (brothers, with an admixture of Canaanitish blood). In this respect they are like their neighbors, the Welsh, the Scots, and the English. The evidence of this startling fact about the Irish is overwhelming, and could fill volumes, though only a small fragment of it can be given here.

The knowledge that the Irish, like the other inhabitants of the British Isles, are Hebrews, has for many centuries been an open secret — by no means the exclusive possession of the British- Israelites, or Anglo-Israelites as they are called in the United States. In Claudius's reign, Pomponius Mela, the Roman geographer, in his *De Situ Orbis* asserted that the Jews were the earliest colonists of Ireland. In the 2nd century, A.D., the Egyptian astronomer, astrologer and geographer Ptolemy wrote: "*Iourna*. They were peopled by the descendants of the Hebrews, and were skilled in smelting operations, and excelled in working metals." Ancient Irish poetry describes the inhabitants of Ireland as "of the race of Heber," — the ancestor of the Hebrews.

The Elizabethan historian Camden, in his *Britannia*, wrote:

> Postellus, in his public lectures in Paris, derives the name Ireland from the Jews, so that *Irin* is quasi *Jurin*, i.e. the land of the Jews. For he says that the Jews, (for-sooth) being the most skilful soothsayers, and presaging that the Empire of the World would at last settle in that strong angle towards the West, took possession of these parts, and of Ireland, very early, and that the Syrians, and the Tyrians also, endeavored to settle themselves there, that they might lay the foundation of a future Empire.

This recalls that it is said of the Welsh that they "call the Irish *Iddew* and the country *Iddewon*, or Jews' land." The Anglo-Israel writer, the Rev. W.H.Poole, in a book published in 1880, comments:

"It is interesting to find this early impartial testimony to a conviction on the Jewish mind of transfer of the Kingdom to the *Isles of the West.* The divine intimation to Jeremiah, to plant a new Kingdom, was, no doubt, the origin of the belief here ascribed to the soothsayers. Camden died 276 years ago, so we see our Israelitish theory then had firm believers among the learned ones.

From the 49th chapter of Isaiah on, the prophet is addressing Israel, and *after* they had become a lost people. He says:

Listen, O Isles, unto me.... Keep silence before me, O Islands.... The Isles shall wait for His law, . . .

Long before the Anglo-Israel theory was ever promulgated it was known that the Isles referred to were the British. As far back as the year 1220, the learned rabbi David Kimchi wrote,

The Islands of the Sea of Isaiah II, belonged (in the past) to the Roman Empire.

In the first quarter of the 18th century, Dr. Abbadie of Amsterdam, after a careful study of the Bible references to Israel in the Isles, wrote,

Unless the ten tribes have flown in the air, or have been plunged to the center of the earth, they must be sought for in the North and West, and in the British Isles.

The Rev. M.S. Bergmann, who translated the Bible into Yiddish, wrote:

I have no hesitation in saying that Great Britain is meant by *the Isles afar off* mentioned by the prophets. This has been opinion of many ancient and modern Jewish theologians. The late Rev. Dr. Margoliouth held, in common with many other Hebrews, that these *Isles* were supposed to have been Britannia, Scotia, and Hibernia.

Hibernians are Hebrews. The great scientist Humboldt was

of the belief that the Irish were anciently of Israel. Tom Moore, Ireland's greatest poet, likened his kinsmen to Jews, and under this impression wrote his immortal *Harp that once through Tara's halls*. The Rev. James McIntosh traced the word Celt, Gael, Cymbri, Engli and Saxon all to their original Hebrew, and said:

> All these races, then — the Danes, Saxons, Angles, Gaels, Celts, Cymbri, and the Northmen, are the Lost Tribes.
> ... We have clearly proved that the place *Arsareth*, to which the Ten Tribes journeyed, was no other than Ireland, a word which is nearer *Erseland* in its form than is Ireland; and that the people of these islands can be identified with the Lost Tribes.

Vallancey, the Protestant Irish historian, says:

> The old language of these islands, was originally Palestine-Scythic: it was in fact the language of that people which Monsieur Bailly calls *L'ancien peuple perdu*. And if I may be allowed the expression, I esteem the Irish, Erse and Manx to be these very ancient people, and therefore they may properly be called *L'ancien peuple perdu, retrouvé*.

The statements of Mela, Ptolemy and Postellus that the Hebrews anciently colonized Ireland are borne out by ancient Jewish and Irish writings and traditions. The old Irish Book of Leinster says: "There were exiles of Hebrew women in Erinn at the coming of the sons of Milesius, who had been driven by a tempest into the ocean by the Tirren Sea. They were in Erinn before the sons of Milesius. They said, however, to the sons of Milesius (who it would appear pressed marriage on them) that they preferred their own country, and that they would not abandon it without receiving dowry for alliance with them. It is from this circumstance that it is the men that purchase wives in Erinn for ever; whilst it is the husbands that are purchased by the wives throughout the world besides." O'Curry, Professor of Irish History and Archaeology in the Catholic University of Ireland, in his *Manners and Customs of the Ancient Irish, volume 2*, says:

> It is stated in very old copies of the *Book of Invasions*, and other ancient documents, that it was the Mosaic law that the Milesians brought into Erinn at their coming; that it had been

learned and received from Moses, in Egypt, by Cae *Cain Breathach*, (Cae, *of the Fair Judgments*), who was himself an Israelite, but had been sent into Egypt to learn the languages of that country by the great Master Fenius Farsaidh, (Fenius *the antiquarian*), from whom the Milesian brothers who conquered Erinn are recorded to have been the 22nd generation in descent; and it is stated in the preface to the Seanchas Mor that this was the law of Erinn at the time of the coming of St. Patrick, in 432.

Camden says that about the time of the Exodus a semitic tribe came to North Ireland. Rabbi Eleazer (Yolkut on Ex.13:17) says they were called out of Egypt by the Lord. Another Jewish author (Medrash, p.51) says they went to Carthage. A third Jewish writer records in Chaldee that they went to Erim The fact that Ireland was so filled with Hebrews was probably the reason the apostles went there. O'Halloran says St. John came to Ireland, and Ussher and Erasmus say St. James visited that land. We recall that Jesus told his disciples to go not to the cities of the gentiles but "rather to the lost sheep of the House of Israel." They seem to have followed instructions.

The Roman Catholic Pinnock wrote a Catechism on the History of Ireland whose questions and answers afford more light on Israel in Erin:

Q: Has any light been thrown upon the other colonies?

A: Yes; a late writer (the author of Precursory Proofs that the Israelites came from Egypt into Ireland, and that the Druids expected the Messiah) has undertaken to show that the formorians were of a higher order than even the Milesians.

Q: Upon what foundation?

A: He asserts that some of the Tribes of Joseph were separated from the Hebrew family at a very early period; that they were heirs of very singular blessings for the latter days, and that they were the Formorians from Africa who had made a settlement in Ireland.

Q: What authority does he produce?

A: Several passages of Scripture, some of the Rabbinical writings, passages of Irish history, certain ancient monuments, coins and customs, and the similarity between the Irish and Hebrew languages.

Q: What language was spoken by the natives?

A: One of very great antiquity, which General Vallancey paid considerable attention to the examination of. It appears to be a compound of the Phoenician and Hebrew, as that learned linguist and antiquarian has not only published several thousand words which are alike in Hebrew and Irish, but has also shown a striking similarity between the Irish and Carthaginian. Then follow passages comparing both languages.

Q: What studies are desirable to promote a knowledge of Irish history?

A: The Hebrew, Chaldaic, Arabic, Phoenician, Irish, and other ancient languages, as well as the few ancient monuments, coins, &c., which remain among the Irish and their descendants in North Britain.

Q: What monuments are remaining?

A: A number of stones, generally twelve in a circle, with one standing in the centre, called Druid circles; such circles abound in Scotland and Ireland, which was anciently the chief seat of Druidism. They also have altar-stones, called cromlechs, on which they sacrifice the firstborn of their flocks." The twelve stones in the circle apparently recalled the great days when the Twelve Tribes of Israel were one nation. As for the altar-stone, an interesting observation is found in the writings of Thomas Moore the historian — not the poet — who says: "It is remarkable that all the ancient altars found in Ireland and now distinguished by the name of Cromleck, or sloping stones, were originally called Bothal, the House of God, and they seem to be of the same species as those mentioned in the Book of Genesis and called by the Hebrews Bethel, which has the same significance as the Irish Bothal."

Dan

Among the Israelites who settled in Ireland was the tribe of Dan in particular. In *The Jew — Our Brother,* I wrote: "Dan was the seafaring tribe of the Israel peoples, and dwelt by the Mediterranean. He and Simeon seem to have been the first tribes to arrive in the British Isles. Dan had a habit of leaving his name around wherever he went, so his travels are easy to trace. Jacob rightly said of him, 'Dan shall be a serpent by the way.' (Gen.49:17) or 'Dan shall be a serpent's trail,' as another translation puts it." DarDaNelles, DANube, DNiester, DNieper — all bodies of water — seem to have been so named by this venturesome tribe. The Danites left their land, sailed to Greece — where they became the renowned and warlike Danai — migrated from Greece in two bodies, one voyaging as far as North Ireland, the other to Denmark — possibly by way of the Danube. "Diodorus Siculus, quoting Hecatoeus of Abdera (6th century B.C.) says:

> The most distinguished of the expelled foreigners (from Egypt) followed Danaus and Cadmus into Greece; but the greater number were led by Moses into Judaea.

Dan's reason for migrating was that he would not fight his brothers, the Jews. Eldad, the eminent Jewish scholar, writes:

> In the days of Jeroboam, Dan refused to shed his brother's blood, and rather than go to war with Judah, he left the country in a body, and went to Greece, to Javan, and to Danmark.

No antisemitism here! Now note that one of the places he settled in was Greece, and that it is in Greece that we hear of a warlike tribe of sea-men known as the Danai, or Dania. Concerning this famous tribe, Dr. Latham, in his *Ethnology of Europe*, says:

> I think that the eponymous of the Argive Dania, was no other than that of the Israelite tribe of Dan.

But Dan travelled farther from Palestine than Greece. Keating, in his *History of Ireland*, states:

> The Danans were a people of great learning and wealth. They left Greece after a battle with the Assyrians and went to Ireland, and Danmark, which they called Dan-mares, Dan's country.

According to *Everyman's Encyclopaedia*, "The Danes claimed origin from Dan," while the ancient *Vetus Chronicon Holsatiae* declares:

> The Danes and Jutes are Jews (Israelites) of the tribe of Dan, and the Angles and Saxons are kindred nations.

As Dan had a habit of giving his dwelling places his own name, it is not surprising that in Ptolemy's map of Ireland we find Dan's Lough, Dan-Sowar, Dan Sobairse, (Dan's resting-place) and Dan-gan castle. Dan's symbol was the serpent, and throughout Ireland and Scotland there have been found strange "serpent mounds."

To sum up about this tribe: Dan migrated to Greece, then to Denmark and Ireland. It is well-known that waves of Danes invaded England, so it is evident that from this one tribe alone the British Isles have taken in a goodly supply of Hebrew blood. No wonder Hitler called Britishers Jews!

Dan was a learned tribe. Therefore it is no surprise that Ireland was a lamp of learning in ancient days. Even English authors have admitted it. Dr. Samuel Johnson says:

> Ireland was at those times the school of the West, the quiet habitation of sanctity and learning.

Frederick Joseph Spencer says:

> We can understand why Ireland was once the light of the world. She was once the asylum and the sanctuary of knowledge, the protectress of the feeble, and the university of the nations.

Says Lord Lyttleton:

> Most of the lights, which, in times past — times of thick darkness, cast their beams over Europe proceeded from Ireland.

Says Sir James Ware:

> The English Saxons received their education from schools then planted in Ireland.

Much did they know, that serpent-tribe of Dan. "Be ye as wise as serpents," says St. Paul. Vallancey observes that

> The Emblem or Symbol of Literature, with the Irish is a tree, or a Serpent, or both: the Tree has been converted to a Club.

Dan was not only learned, but psychic too. Vallancey records that

> The tuatha (tribe) de Danaan were called Oinin, Ainin, meaning soothsayers in Irish. The Hebrew prophets were called Anan, meaning "he covered with a cloud."

Our Irish Oinin were remarkable for having the power of raising a thick fog at their pleasure. Hence Ireland was called Inis anan or the Island of Prophets.

Our Da Danans being settled in the county of Donegal, the country was called Tir-oin or the country of Oin and they were named Treabh-pin or Treavoin, the tribe of Oin or sorcerers. It is said they brough with them from Egypt to Greece and so to Ireland a stone called Leabadea or the altar of destiny, otherwise Liagfail the stone of fate, known also by the name of Cloch na Cineamhna, properly Kinana, on which the Irish and Scots kings were wont to be crowned; now in Westminster Abbey....Fal and fail in Irish is fate, destiny. Ireland was named Inis-fail and Inis-anan the island of fate, the island of soothsayers.

As Hebrew-speaking Dan knew magic, many Irish words pertaining to sorcery are from the Hebrew. Here are a few:

English	Hebrew	Irish
To divine	kasam	geasam
A sorcerer	ounan,anan	oinin
An enchanter	nahhash	neas
A charmer	cheber	geabhar
A knowing one	iadanani	Deadanan

On this last word, inset with the name of the tribe itself, Vallancey comments:

> The old Irish wrote it also with the sound of the Hebrew Y, *dagne*.

The Irish priests (Druids), who were as monotheistic as Moses, had another name for themselves. They used the term *Ceadruicht* , i.e. "the inspiration of the Holy Spirit." The Hebrew *kodesruach* has the same meaning. And as servants of God, or ministers, they called themselves *sruth*, i.e. clergy, or ministers. *Shiruth* in Hebrew has the same meaning. (Exodus 24:13)

Dan and the other Israelites and Judahites who came to Erin left many signs of their presence there. Dan in placenames, and the serpent-mounds have already been mentioned. Other place-names are significant. Previous to their captivity,

Baal-worship was the besetting sin of the Israelites. Many of their towns and places were named after this god, as for instance,

Baal-Be-Rith, Baal-Gad, Baal-Hamon,
Baal-Ha-Nan, Baal-Ha-zar,Baal-Peor,
Baal-Me-On, Baal-Lah, Baal-Lath, Baale,
Baali, Baalis.

This name is as frequently found in Ireland:

Baal-y-Bai, Baal-y-Gowan, Baal-y-Nahinsh, Baal-y-Castell, Baal-y-Moni, Baal-y-Ner, Baal-y-Garai, Baal-y-Nah, Baal-y-Con-El, Baal-y-Hy, Baal-y-Hull-Ish, Baal-Nah-Brach, Baal-Athi, Baal- Dagon

"Till very recent times," says Professor Otte, in his *Scandinavian History*, p.5, "the country people in some parts of Ireland and Scotland, and even of England, had the custom of celebrating the return of midsummer-night on the 24th of June, by dancing together round a large fire lighted on some high hill, or running three times through the fire to secure the fulfilment of a wish. These midsummernight dances, which were known in Britain as *Bel-tanes*, are nothing but the remains of an earlier form of Baal-worship."

The Harp of David

There are indications that the prophet Jeremiah came to Ireland after the destruction of the Kingdom of Judah, uprooted Baal-worship in the land, and established at Tara (Heb. *Torah*, the Law) a law-dispensing center for the realm.

With him he may have brought the Harp of David, and it is believed by many that this very harp is hidden in the mysterious and yet-to-be-opened mound of Tara. Perhaps this matter will not be known until, as old Irish prophecy says, the mound is opened "by one whose cognomen is the Red" (Ruadh). Be this as it may, the Irish use the Harp of David symbolically. In a book entitled *Dialogue on Ancient and Modern Music*, (1581) by Vincentio Galilei, the father of the great astronomer, we read of the Irish Harp:

This most ancient instrument was brought to us from Ireland

(as Dante says) where they are excellently made, and in great numbers, the inhabitants of that island having practised on it for many and many ages. Nay, they even place it in the arms of the kingdom, and paint it on their public buildings, and stamp it on their coin, giving as the reason, their being descended from the royal prophet David.

Edward Hine writes:

The harp must have been dear to every true Israelite....The songs of David and his skill on the harp must have rendered it the most precious heir-loom in his family....It is a lawful question to ask, How came the harp on the royal standard? How was it that Ireland became at so early a period so famous for the *harp* and the science of music, so as to become the teacher of both Scotland and Wales?" (Today it is still the most popular instrument in the Israel lands — and elsewhere — for the piano is the Harp of David boxed.) "That the harp should be found on the British Standard, which bears the very emblems of Judah and Israel, with the young lions thereof, does seem, indeed, to identify the harp with the praises of the sweet singer of Israel, and the Divine glory that once shone around it on the holy hill of Zion. Therefore, the transplanted sacred service by the Prophet Jeremiah, together with the royal associations of the house of David, must, we think, have been the means of the fame for the harp and music for which Ireland was so celebrated in those far, very far back times, when the foundations of the great kingdom of Israel were laid in the British Islands, and the sovereignty of the seed of David on that wonderful stone; who, famous as he was as a warrior, in the sight of men, was still more famous in the sight of God, as the sweet singer of Israel, and a man after God's own heart.

The harp is immensely significant in its symbolism. As the Anglo- Israel writer, Morton Spencer says:

The fifth empire that Daniel saw which became a mountain "and filled the whole earth", we have fully followed to the British Islands which is to form the *nucleus* for the world-wide empire over which the Heir of David will reign....There is to be another ruling David, who will consolidate the Hebrew empire as the first David had done (Ezek.37:23-24). Then the government may be overturned to Jerusalem....After the never-to-be-relinquished union of Judah and Israel in the Holy Land, it is said: "David my servant shall be king over them."

Irish and Hebrew

One of the names of the land where David's Harp was brought is Hibernia. This name may mean "Hebrew land." The Irish themselves claim descent from Heber, the ancestor of the Hebrews. Vallancey writes:

> From hence may be derived the name Iber or Hiber, in like manner as the children of Abraham, from passing over the Euphrates, were called Hebrews; and it is remarkable, that if the Irish Seannachies have imposed upon us, in the date when their ancestors took the name of Heber, they have done it with great art and cunning, making it correspond with that of the Hebrews.

At any rate Hebrew is the language of the Irish.

Inscriptions in ancient Hebrew have been found throughout the Emerald Isle. According to Sir Joseph Ware, some have been dug up at Clonmacknoise. Hebrew and Irish are so much alike that the scholar Muir states: "The Erse of Ireland, the Gaelic of Scotland and the Kymric of Wales, come from a dialect of early Hebrew." Vallancey says: "The language of the early inhabitants of Ireland was a compound of Hebrew and Phoenician." And again, he says: "So great an affinity has the old Irish with the Hebrew, that my friend and correspondent, J.J.Heideck, Professor of Oriental languages, will not be persuaded, but that a Jewish colony once settled in Ireland."

A few words that are the same in both languages have already been given in this chapter. Here are more:

English	Hebrew	Irish
Judge	Dan	Dunn
Lord	Ab	Ab
Father,dad	dod	daid
Woman	Bahin	Ban
Old woman	calach	cailliac
Son	bar	bar
Society	Sanhedrim	saindrean
Heaven	Zion	Sion
Granary	Schibol	sciobal

Feather	chloim	clum
Fire	ur	ur
Sun	Baal	Baal,Bel
Sun-fire,fire	Moloch	molc
Moon	chiun	cann
Oracle	iod	iodh
Sacrifice	katir	ceitern
Mixed people	mesk	meask
Merchants	chananaei	chanaidhe
Ship	Gnabhara	cnabbra
Bark	barichim	barc
Mariner	melach	Meilachoir
To float	naah	naibh
Water,To drink	hiskah	uisce
Covenant	berit	berit
Meridian sun	darom	daram
East	kadim	keadmus
West	ahor	jorar
North	shemol	sumbail
South	jamin	imheaoin

O'Hart, in his *Irish Pedigrees*, says:

As showing an affinity between the Irish and the Hebrew languages, it may be remarked that the Irish pronoun *se* signifies *he, him,* and that the Hebrew pronoun *se* also means *he, him*; that the Irish pronoun *so,* which means *this* or *that,* is like the Hebrew *so,* which has the same meaning; and that the Irish pronoun *isi,* always expressed to signify *a female,* is analogous to the Hebrew *isa,* which means *a woman.*

Mac

Vallancey explains: "*Mac,* a son. The Irish have all the Hebrew words for a son, viz. *nin, manon, shilo, bar, and ben,* but this word *mac* is applied in the same manner as the Hebrew *zacar* a male child, because, say the Cabbalists, the word signifies memory, which is as much as to say, the memory of the father is preserved in the son; according to that speech of Absalom, I have no son to keep my name in remembrance; *Mac* in the old Irish implies a remembrance, hence *mactaim* in the

111

modern, to ponder, to weigh the memory: in Hebrew *imecha*, to approve on recollection.... In the Irish text, at the beginning of this section we have *macraith*, i.e. youthful males. This word occurs in Gen.xlix:5 The English version has it translated habitations. Montanus, dubious of the word, inserts the Hebrew in the Latin text, in Italicks, thus, 'arma iniquitatis eorum machara.' Rabbi Meir who lived in the time of the second temple, gives another turn to the whole verse. 'By the blessing of Jacob upon Simon and Levi, the weapons of vengeance are their *machirothim* children.' 'That is,' says he, 'they love weapons as their children: and hence,' adds he, *mak* and *makir* is a son, and the words are used by the inhabitants of the sea coasts, and in the cities on those coasts.'"

Goimh

Vallancey explains: "*Goimh*. Vexation, affliction, hate, malice, a grudge; this is a very extraordinary word. In the Irish it implies also a tribe which you pity and hate, as *goimhar;* for which reason it is sometimes written for *gudh*, to signify a battle, a fight; the latter is the Hebrew *gad* and *gadadh*, to assault, to attack, so is *goimh* the Hebrew *goim,* the Gentiles, that is, all nations but that of the Israelites."

Shalom

Vallancey says: "The salutation of the Irish at parting is *slan leact* or *leat*, i.e.peace and health be with you; this is evidently a corruption of the Hebrew *shalom lach*, the ordinary salutation of the Jews, and which is used by our Saviour, in the gospel, to his disciples. The root in Hebrew is *shalam*, he was perfected, or made perfect; the Irish *slan* has the same signification....*Leacht* is the proper word, when implying to take in the hand, or about you, in possession, as *beir leachd sin*, take that (thing) with you. *Lacad* in Hebrew, signifies the action of taking with the hand....Sometimes they say *Sith-leat* or *Si-leat*, i.e. peace be with you; this is the Hebrew *Selati*: the burial service of the Jews is thus, 'Let his soul be bound in the garden of Eden. Amen, Amen, Amen.' 'Selati.'"

"*Sela*, found in the Psalms of Praise, is also an Irish word expressing 'every praise and thanksgiving that can be given by the creature to the Creator.'"

Breith-Neam

"Covenant" in Hebrew is *brit*, or *berit*. In Irish it is *berit*.
"Heaven, heavenly" is in Hebrew, *nam*; in Irish, *neam*. Vallancey says of the Covenant of Heaven:

> The Breith(pl.) neamh was revised triennially at Tarah,
> where all the states of the kingdom were assembled. The name
> of the place seems to have been given from Torah, lex, the law;
> and at this assembly we read of a feast given to the people. This
> was probably a sacrifice; for with the ancients no covenant was
> made or ratified without a sacrifice.

McCabe

According to O'Hart: "The derivation of the name Maccabees
seems to be the same as that of the Irish surname MacCabe;
namely *caba*, which is Irish for a cape, a cap, or hood; while
the Hebrew *Kaba* has the same meaning."

Iodhan Morain

O'Hart says: "The Druidic Irish had Hebraic customs to a
great extent: for instance — the Druidic judges were of a priestly
caste, and wore each a collar of gold. Buxtorf states that this
collar was called *Iodhan Morain;* and *Iodhan Morain* is Chaldee
for Urim and Thummim (see Exodus xxviii:30) Whether it was
the Gaels who borrowed that Mosaic badge from the Israelites,
or that it was the Israelites who borrowed it from the Gaels,
we cannot say; but *iodhan Morain* is also Gaelic, and as such
is said to be so called after a celebrated Irish brehon who lived
in the first century of the Christian era." Vallancey was so
startled by the survival in Ireland of the high-priest's breast-
plate that he wrote a Rabbi friend in London for further information. The Rabbi replied that the expression was Jewish, and
proved it by Talmudic quotations. For instance, Rabbi Joda in
Talmud Sanhedrim, named the breast-plate *Ioden Moren*.
Vallancey comments on the use of the *Iodhan Morain*:

The High Priest was not to consult the Ruim for any private person, but only for the king, for the president of the Sanhedrim, for the general of an army, or for some other great prince or public governor in Israel; and not for any private affairs, but for such only as related to the public interest of the nation, either in Church or State.

Our Hibernian Druids never consulted the *Iodhan Morain*, but in the courts of justice, or on affairs of state; to all their decrees *urraim*, i.e. implicit obedience was paid.

In dubious cases, or where the interest of the Church was concerned, or the election of a king, they consulted the *Liath Meisicith*, or *Liath Fail*." (Now in Westminster Abbey.)

Sometimes, working back from the Irish to the Hebrew has been helpful in explaining or elucidating obscure words in the older language. According to Vallancey: "The Irish language can explain the meaning of two words in the Hebrew, which have perplexed all commentators, and were very probably Pelasgian or Scythian words introduced by the Scythopolians into Palestine: I mean the *Keri* and *Ketib*, the names of the marginal notes of the Bible, inserted by the Masorae, or as some rabbies will have it, by Ezras.

In another essay on ancient Irish history, Vallancey relates that

. . . religious customs and ceremonies, borrowed by the Jews from the idolatrous nations in the East, are often expressed by a single word, the true signification of which is not to be found in the Hebrew, Chaldean, or Arabic languages: the same words are frequently to be met in the Irish MSS. denoting the same ceremony, and this so described, as to leave no room for conjecture; for example, *Samac, Smac,* or *Smag,* in Irish, is the palm of the hand: at the coronation of a king, or the ordination of a Priest, the Chief Priest passed the palms of both hands down the temples of the Prince or Priest, and he was then said to be *smac'd*; hence *smacd* or *smact*, signifying authority; one set over the people; *crioch-smacd*, a government, from *crioch*, a Territory; and as a verb, *smacdam* is to govern. The same word is used by Moses, when he put Joshua in authority, with the same ceremony. 'And Joshua the Son of Nun was full of the spirit of wisdom; for Moses *samach'd* him, laying his hands upon him: and the Children of Israel hearkened unto him, and did as the Lord commanded Moses.' A second example is in the Irish word *amarcall*, i.e. Signum X, that is, the sign with which the Emir, or Noble, was anointed on the forehead between the eyes: it is the ancient Hebrew, Samaritan, and Irish X Thau; and hence arose the office of the Jewish Priests called *immorcalim*, or *Immarcalin*.

Other Resemblances

He says again: "Our Hibernian Druids always wore a key, like the law doctors of the Jews, to shew they alone had the key of the sciences, i.e. that they alone could communicate the knowledge of the doctrine they preached. The name of this key was *kire* or *cire*, (and *eo*, a peg or pin, being compounded with it, forms the modern *eo-cire*, the key of a lock.) A comment, correction, remark or explanation of a writing was named *kire ceo keatfa*, i.e. the key and explanation of the sense (of the author;) these words are certainly corrupted from the Chaldee *keri ou ketib*."

In his *Essay on Irish Festivals,* Vallancey writes:

The Pentecost of the Jews is a high festival observed by them in memory of the promulgation of the law from mount Sinai, and also a giving thanks to God for the return of the harvest, and this festival has three names in Hebrew, one of which is *chag kalzir*, solemnitas messis, a day they observe lacteis cibis, ut scriblitis and libis vescuntur, eo quod lex, tum temporis ipsis data, alba instar lactis fuerit. (See Buxtorf, in Synag.c.20 & Leusden's Philolog. Hebraeo.p.275.) The Irish still keep this day as in times of heathenism with lacteis cibis, & c. And although it is not the season of harvest in this climate, yet according to the custom of their Oriental-Scytho-polian ancestors, the breakfast on Whitsunday is always composed of cake bread, and the white liquor drunk with it, is made of hot water poured on *wheaten* bran, which they call *caingaos* (or kingeesh from the day) and this liquor is also frequently made in time of harvest for the workmen in the field.

Under the heading, *The Gaelic Land System Same as that of the Hebrews,* O'Hart comments:

Even in the matter of the Gaelic system of allotting a portion of land to each head of a family for the sustenance of himself and those dependent on him (and which obtained among the Gaels in Ireland down to the 17th century, in the reign of King

James I of England), how strangely coincident was that Gaelic system with the Land System of the Hebrews. 'And ye shall divide the land by lot for an inheritance among your families: and to the more ye shall give the more inheritance, and to the fewer ye shall give the less inheritance: every man's inheritance shall be in the place where his lot falleth; according to the tribes of your fathers ye shall inherit.' See also Nos. 26:54-56, & Josh. 11:23, 24, & 26, etc. This similarity between the Land System of the Irish Gaels and that which obtained among the Hebrews is the more extraordinary, when we consider the intimacy which existed between Moses and Gaodhal (gael). But we are unable to say which (if either) of these two ancient people gave their Land System to the other.

Professor Sullivan, noting the kinship between the English and Irish, says:

The results which I have obtained...throw an unexpected light on the early institutions of the Anglo-Saxons, and upon the origin of the English representative system.... In comparing the Irish political and social systems with those of adjacent countries, I have almost invariably referred to Anglo-Saxon England, and hardly ever to France, the head-quarters of the so-called Kelts.... All the fundamental principles of Anglo-Saxon law existed among the Britons and Irish." He speaks of the "most special connection of their languages, the result either of long-continued unity or of a very special relationship of the mind of the peoples.

A relationship between the laws of the ancient British and the Hebrews was noted by Frederick J. Spencer, in his lecture to the London Anthropological Society:

Civil law enacted that a brother was bound to marry his brother's widow, and so raise up children to his brother. Now I maintain that this is conclusive, as no other Tribe in the world's history, save the Hebrew Tribes, had such a law as this. The Ecclesiastical law enacted Tithes, after the Israelitish form, and they were in force until Cardinal Parpro's arrival in Ireland, when he swept this, and many other Israelitish laws, away.

This is only a small fragment of the evidence that the Irish are of Israel. A bulky book could be crammed with further facts as weighty. But if the Irish are of Israel, so are the other dwellers in the Isles. And so are the Scandinavians, the Dutch, the

Americans, and other peoples. In the latter days — now upon us — the mighty millions of today's Twelve Tribes are to re-unite to form the Stone Kingdom of prophecy that is to cover the earth. Turn to the Bible, which foretells the whole story. So what is our duty as Christians and Israelites? It is to look for likenesses and not differences, for harmonies and not discords, to seek and find Israel wherever Israel may be found. Unite Israel and the rest of the world is united. Holy Writ says:

> When the Most High divided to the nations their inheritance, when he separated the sons of Adam, he set the bounds of the people according to the number of the children of Israel.

So when Israel is restored, all things will be restored. Bring together the Lost Tribes *and* the Jews, under the leadership of the House of Joseph, and the Golden Age and the Millennium will arrive. The Irish, English, Scots, Welsh and Jews, who are literally, racially brothers, form the strongest stock of a mighty tree, that described in Scandinavian mythology as the World Tree of Yggdrasil — that is, Israel. The world as it is today is a scattered jig-saw puzzle, but to learn the identity of Israel is to put the pieces together and reveal the wondrous picture of this beneficent all-shadowing Tree whose roots run into the earth and whose summit lives in Heaven.

"Anglo-Israel Is Marching Under Orders"
(Mary Baker Eddy)

The principal pillar of peace for the the imminent New Age is *Anglo-American Unity*. *This becomes Anglo-American-Jewish Unity*, for in these latter days, Scripture says, "Judah will walk to Israel." This unity will be won; and when it is, wakened by the collective right-thinking of men and women of vision, it will be followed up by borders enlarged to include all Europe and finally the yellow and dark races.

First the spiritual and racial identity of the children of God will be revealed in lightning flashes of truth. Then Israel everywhere will learn that it has a task: to promote unity among the races by the revealing of relationships. When these relationships (and not differences) begin to be uncovered, others will be found, and when these are traced, still others will be brought to light. Finally the entire interlocking racial pattern of mankind will stand revealed as a single organism, a living and breathing body. Then will be seen in all its glory the mighty world tree of Yggdrasil or Israel. All mankind will be recognized as Israel, either by race or by adoption. With no one excluded, for "they shall all know Me, from the least of them unto the greatest." And to know God is to be a prince of God. And to be a prince of God is to be an Israelite. Thus by continuous revelation the Stone Kingdom will grow and spread until it covers the earth.

But where does that Kingdom begin that is never to end? Where is that rock that is cut out of the mountains without hands? Some Scripture students know the answer. They have discovered that the nucleus, basis, and foundation of the devouring Stone Kingdom of prophecy is Great Britain, a literal kingdom of stone whose very name is Albion or "White Cliffs." Here is a truth that is palpable, overwhelming, wonderful. Even William Blake who seems to have known nothing of the truth that the English are literally Israel, nevertheless somehow sensed that Britain was at once Israel and the Stone Kingdom of prophecy. In his *Jerusalem* he proclaimed in prophet voice:

> They came up to Jerusalem: they walked before Albion:
> In the exchanges of London every Nation walk'd,
> And London walk'd in every Nation, mutual in love and harmony.
> Albion cover'd the whole Earth, England encompass'd the Nations.
> Mutual each within other's bosom in Visions of Regeneration.

But God in His wisdom has not decreed that Britain is to serve alone in her governance of Israel. Her rebel offshoot and kin are included in the rule. The House of Joseph is to govern the royal race. The two tribes or peoples constituting the House of Joseph are Ephraim and Manasseh. Britain is Ephraim. The United States is Manasseh. Ephraim had a standard with a Bull or a Unicorn as crest. Manasseh was tribe number thirteen - the number of America - and we are told:

> The Jewish Talmudists gave the eagle symbol to Manasseh because of its affinity to his name. The Hebrew root of the word 'Manasseh' conceals the root of another Hebrew word, *Nesher* or *Neshar*, an *eagle*.

And in the two greatest cities of the lands of John Bull and of the Eagle are the two obelisks, which represent the land that was ruled by Joseph, and from which they were taken, and now you know too why Egypt's pyramid is on America's Coat of Arms. Here is *union now*, divinely destined.

History Of The Vision

First mention of the prophetic history of the House of Israel is found in the 48th chapter of Genesis, where we find described two great segments of Israel, Britain-Ephraim, and America-Manasseh:

> And Israel stretched out his right hand, and laid it upon Ephraim's head, who was the younger and his left hand upon

119

Manasseh's head, crossing his hands wittingly; for Manasseh was the firstborn. And he blessed Joseph and said . . . God . . . bless the lads . . . and let them grow into a multitude in the midst of the earth. The firstborn (Manasseh) . . . he also shall become a people (the U.S.A.) . . . and he also shall be great; howbeit his younger brother (Ephraim) shall be greater than he and his seed shall become a multitude of nations. And he blessed them that day, saying, In thee shall Israel bless.

Some will say here that Manasseh-America is a younger nation than Britain; so they should note that in the above prophecy the *individual* Manasseh is spoken of, who is to *become* a great people. And elsewhere the Bible has "Ephraim is my firstborn."

Inspired prophecy fulfills itself. Israel grew into an immense multitude, became a mighty kingdom, but grew corrupt and so suffered subjugation, was made captive by the Assyrians, later escaped, and migrated in a north and westerly direction to the Scandinavian peninsula and also to the "Isles" as Angles, Saxons, Jutes, Normans, Danes, etc. And here in the Rock Realm of Albion the seed of Israel increased, spread out and abroad, to become the multitude or company of nations prophesied by Jacob. And when Israel in the Isles raised the standard of Ephraim the hand of God was seen again, for the flag was the Union Jack, and Union Jack means Union of Jacob or Union of Israel.

The Lord of Abraham and Isaac promised Jacob: "Thy seed shall be as the dust of the earth, and thou shalt spread abroad to the west, and to the east, and to the north, and to the south." (Gen. 28:14) The prophecy has been fulfilled. British Israel's first colonizing move was to Newfoundland (1583 A.D.), west of Palestine and Britain. Her next was to India, east of Palestine and Britain. Later came Australia, south of Palestine and Britain.

The expansion of the British Empire began soon after the Union Jack was raised. The early seventeenth century saw the rise to power of Oliver Cromwell, the Puritan dictator who knew so well both how to praise the Lord and pass the ammunition. This Bible-toting warrior was a true Israelite. When Rabbi Manasseh ben Israel (note the name!) came to England to solicit the Jews' readmission to the land, Cromwell granted the request. Thereafter many of the Jews looked upon Cromwell as the Messiah, and even made fruitless enquiries to ascertain if he were of Jewish stock. And from the time that the Protector invited the Jews back to England, hoping thereby to build upon the country and forward the millennium, England began to grow great as an Empire.

In Cromwell's twenty-first year the Puritan Empire of ManassehAmerica was born, for in 1620 a little band of Pilgrim Fathers left the rocky Isles of Albion for the western wilderness. Did not Isaiah foresee it:

> The children which thou shalt have, after thou hast lost the other, shall say again in thine ears, The place is too strait for me: give place to me that I may dwell.

The Displacement Factor

A hundred and fifty years passed. Manasseh grew mighty, independent-minded, and cocky. Ephraim,now a powerful Empire, was lax, lackadaisical, and arrogant towards her American colonies. The Americans were almost independent anyway. They were allowed to defy the navigation laws, and did so exultantly. The old voluntary system of taxation was popular in the colonies. But some colonies gave large amounts, others little or none. This caused wrangling, and England wanted a more orderly system. A stamp tax would bear equally on all. According to the American historian Fisher the stamp tax was fair: "It was the sort of tax we levied on ourselves during the Civil War, and again at the time of the war with Spain." Then, "England, with a population of eight million, was in debt to the tune of $148,000,000. The colonies had no taxes except light ones. Why shouldn't they shoulder part of the load?"

However, Ephraim unjustly insisted upon taxation without representation, and Manasseh rightly resisted. But it was a family squabble, with - as Frank Knox has said - "probably more champions of American Independence in England itself than on this side of the water." And when America in 1766 refused to submit to the Stamp Tax, William Pitt exclaimed in Parliament: "I rejoice that America has resisted... If ever this nation should have a tyrant for a King, six millions of free men, so dead to all the feelings of liberty as voluntarily to submit to be slaves, would be fit instruments to make slaves of the rest." And Horace Walpole expressed a common British point of view: "I rejoice that the Americas are to be free, as they had a right to be, and as I am sure they have shown they deserve to be."

Indeed, so many Britishers were against war with America that had it not been for German King George's fake Parliament "largely elected by fake votes" the British people would not have been dragged into the war. As it was, so few Britishers could be persuaded to fight those of their own blood that the German King had to hire Hessians to help him out.

It was an unfortunate quarrel, and no wonder that Nostradamus, the French descendant of Israel prophesied of it sorrowfully:

The Occident will be free of the British Isles, Not satisfied, sad rebellion!

Further shattering blows were struck. Again Israel fought itself. In 1812 John Bull unjustly impressed American soldiers, just as 79 years later American sailors unjustly seized Canadian vessels in the Behring Sea sixty miles offshore. In 1812 the British burned Washington, just as the year before the Americans had burned Toronto.[1]

Later in the century evil forces were still trying to prevent the realization of Abraham's vision. Civil war came. The envious elements of disunity induced Britain to side largely with the confederacy and to adopt a policy which the people of Ephraim later regretted. There were also war-threats over the Northwestern boundary.

The union of Manasseh-Israel was preserved by a great Abraham (no chance coincidence in that patriarchal name), but the devils of disunity and jingoism seemed to be pulling America and Britain farther apart. In 1895 war over the Venezuelan Boundary dispute seemed inevitable. As Christmas approached, Wall Street and the yellow press were clamoring for war. Even President Cleveland was mesmerized. The New York World stood almost alone against the clamor. The Jew Joseph Pulitzer cabled leaders of British opinion and got reassuring answers. Sanity was restored and the war clouds vanished. People then realized that Britain and America were too closely related ever to go to war against each other again. And thus the long-prophesied reunion moved a step nearer its inevitable realization.

Then came the Spanish-American war of 1898, and again evil forces were tempting the British to take the wrong side of the anti-Israel controversy. Over a century before, a German king and German soldiers had opposed America, and history now repeated itself. German agents approached Mr. Balfour, proposing that Ephraim join a European combination against us. But Mr. Balfour was a true Israelite, and refused.

On its way from Spain to Manila through the Suez Canal a formidable part of the Spanish navy stopped for coal at Port Said. The law regarding the coaling of belligerent warships in neutral ports could have been construed against us. Lord Cromer construed it in such a way that it worked in our favor. The Spanish ships could not get to Manila Bay in time to take part against Admiral Dewey. They had been given only, enough coal to carry them to Barcelona!   In April, 1898, an interesting scene occurred at the British Embassy in Washington. The representatives of the various European nations dropped in for a visit to the British Ambassador. They had just come from the German Embassy, where they all had signed a document hostile to the United States. Would the British Ambassador please affix *his* august name to it? He read it, then remarked, "I have no orders from my government to sign any such document as that. And if I did have, I should resign my post rather than sign it."

In England, Earl Grey suggested quietly to John Hay, the American Ambassador in London, "Why do not the States borrow our navy to make a quick job of Cuba? They could return us the favor another time." And in this period of crisis for America, Joseph Chamberlain said,

> Shoulder to shoulder, we could command peace the world over.

Better than "commanding" peace, however, is bringing people together by pulling harmony down from heaven. Exhibit A may be Walter Lippman's *American Foreign Policy*, which has done much to change the attitude of many Americans towards co-operation with Great Britain. His book has swayed even the policy of the republicans of Mackinack Island. With the invincible logic of sound documentary evidence Lippman demonstrated that the Founding Fathers were anything but isolationists and that they foresaw dangers that are still to come. Washington rejoiced when Franklin succeeded in winning the King of France as an ally, and he welcomed the support of Holland and Russia. In the matter of the Louisiana Purchase, Jefferson was most happy to have the diplomatic encouragement of Britain. In the preparation of the Monroe Doctrine the decision was made only after negotiations in London, by which America was assured of the armed diplomatic support of the Old Country. Jefferson even believed it might be necessary for us to:

> Marry ourselves to the British fleet and nation. . . .
> . . . Great Britain is the nation which can do us the most harm of any one, or all on earth; and with her on our side we need not fear the whole world.

Madison used like language:

> With the British power and navy combined with our own, we have nothing to fear from the rest of the world.

An American woman prophet, who was born before these two Founding Fathers died articulated a similar hope for Union Now. This woman, the Discoverer and Founder of Christian Science, was Mary Baker Eddy. She was passionately pro-British.[1] In the early Christian Science Sentinel, which was under her personal supervision, articles frequently appeared which urged a better understanding of and closer cooperation with Britain. Lady Mildred Fitzgerald reports that in her conversations with Mrs. Eddy the Christian Science leader manifested a strong desire for ever closer bonds between Britain and America.

A momentous event brought Mrs. Eddy's feelings to the fore. When trouble brewed in Manila Bay between the aggressive German Admiral Diedrich and Admiral Dewey, who was policing the place, Diedrich chose his own spot to anchor. "At last, it is reported, Dewey told him that if he wanted trouble, he could have it, 'at the drop of a hat.' Then Diedrich called on the English Admiral, likewise anchored in Manila Bay. 'What would you do,' enquired the German, 'in the event of trouble between Admiral Dewey and myself?' 'That is a secret known only to Admiral Dewey and me,' answered the Englishman. Next morning the British cruiser in a new place, interposed between Dewey and the German Admiral. The Kaiser's squadron sailed off fuming. Late that year, when it was all over, the furious Kaiser wrote to a friend of Joseph Chamberlain, 'If I had had a larger fleet I would have taken Uncle Sam by the scruff of the neck.'"

Our best friend during this crisis was John Bull. "There was an outburst of European hate for us, " writes Owen Wister. "Germany, France and Austria all looked expectantly to England — and England disappointed their expectations. The British press was as much for us as the French and German press were hostile; the London Spectator said: 'We are not, and we do not pretend to be, an agreeable people, but when there is trouble in the family, we know where our hearts are.'"

One noteworthy expression of British goodwill for us appeared in the London Chronicle for April 22, 1898, under the initials W.A. This was the poem that prompted Mrs. Eddy's prophetic reply. W.A. wrote:

America, dear brother land!
While yet the shotted guns are mute,
Accept a brotherly salute,
A hearty grip of England's hand.

Tomorrow, when the sulphurous glow
Of war shall dim the stars above,
Be sure the star of England's love
Is over you, come weal or woe.

Go forth in hope! Go forth in might!
To all your nobler self be true,
That coming times may see in you
The vanguard of the hosts of light.

Though wrathful justice load and train
Your guns, be ev'ry breach they make
A gateway pierced for mercy's sake
That peace may enter in and reign.

Then should the hosts of darkness band
Against you, lowering thund'rously,
Flash the word, Brother o'er the sea
And England at your side shall stand

Exulting! For though dark the night
And sinister the scud and rack,
The hour that brings us back to back
But harbingers the larger light.

When this poem came to the attention of Mary Baker Eddy, she was already an ardent devotee of Anglo-Israel truth. That Britain and America are Israel and that they must and will reunite for the salvation of themselves and of all humanity was a belief that had won her ready sympathy and acceptance. Hence it is not surprising that W.A.'s verses met with such hearty reciprocation. She replied prophetically in a poem entitled:

The United States to Great Britain

Hail, brother! fling thy banner
To the billows and the breeze;
We proffer thee warm welcome
With our hand, though not our knees . . .

The hoar fight is forgotten;
Our eagle, like the dove,
Returns to bless a bridal
Betokened from above.

That "Union Now" would come Mrs. Eddy knew well, for she prophesied a "bridal" for the nations named in the title of her poem, and a bridal is a wedding or marriage.

"List, brother!" angels whisper
To Judah's sceptred race, —
"Thou of the self-same spirit,
Allied by nation's grace,

Wouldst cheer the hosts of heaven;
For Anglo-Israel, lo!
Is marching under orders;
His hand averts the blow."

Brave Britain, blest America!
Unite your battle-plan;
Victorious, all who live it —
The love for God and man.

To understand the full import and thrust of this poem one needs a little knowledge of the Anglo-Israel key to Bible prophecy and the terminology of this illumination. For instance:

"Anglo-Israel is marching under orders." "Lost" Israel is today the inhabitants of the British Isles and their offspring, together with the Scandinavian and Celtic peoples, with their diverse pockets, scattered throughout the world. Ephraim-Britain and Manasseh-America, the principal powers are marching under orders towards a divinely pre-ordained *unity*, that is, towards a giant benevolent and beneficent federation. It is coming: "Our eagle returns....to bless a bridal betokened from above." Jefferson, who announced that someday it might be necessary for the American eagle to marry the British Empire, did not go as far in thought as Mr. Eddy, who affirms the American Eagle should return to England and that such a marriage or bridal is inevitable, because "betokened from above."

Our eagle will return to "Judah's sceptred race." This is British-Israel, still "ruled over" today by a lineal descendant of King David of the House of Judah. The rulers of Israel were crowned by the stone known as Jacob's pillow, which accompanied the prophet Jeremiah and his scribe Baruch to Ireland, to the town of Tara (Torah) the law-giving center of the realm. Thence to Scone in Scotland, and finally to Westminster Abbey, where the rock pillow is now known as "the Stone of Scone."

It is not only the Bible that predicts an Anglo-Israel federation: it is plainly stated in Nostradamus. In quatrain 10:66 (Is that a symbolic date too?) he pens:

There will be a head of London from the government of America
Island of Scotland, he will pave you with ice;
They will have Reb for king, a very false Antichrist,
Who will put them all into an uproar.

Le chef de Londres par regne l'Americh,
L'Isle d'Écosse t'empiera par gelée;
Roy Reb auront, un si faux Antechrist.
Qui les mettra trestous dans la meslée.

To my knowledge Nostradamus was the first man in the world to write down in cool print the words

government of America.

When he wrote, there was no government of America, nor would there be for years to come.

Who or what Reb means we cannot yet know. Then what is a "false Antichrist," and a very false one? A false Christ would be an antichrist. It has been suggested the expression means one wrongly accused of being an antichrist. Time will tell.

Another Nostradamus quatrain seems to relate to the same event:

Within the Isles a very horrible tumult,
Nothing will be heard but a clashing of factions,
The harm wrought by the brigands will be so great,
That one will have to take his place in the great league.

Dedans les isles si horrible tumulte,
Rien on n'orra qu'une belligue brigue,
Tant grand sera des prediteurs l'insulte,
Qu'on se viendra ranger á la grand ligue. (2.100)

Many British and many Americans will resist any thought of subordination of their lands to a federation. But this gigantic event has been foreseen not only by the prophets of the Bible and by Nostradamus, but by seers of many times and times.

Here is one vision from Thomas the Rhymer (1220-1297):

A bastard shall come out of the west,
Not in England borne shall he be....
He shall into Ynglond ryde,
And holde a parliament of moche pryde,
That never (such) parlament byfore was syne,
And false lawes he shall leye (put) downe,
That are goyng in that countre;
And true workes he shall begyn,

And alle leder of bretane shall he be...

A bastard in wedlock born shall come out of the west,
A chiftane unchosen that shall choose for himself,
And ride through the realm, and Roy shall be called...
A chiftane stable as a stone, stedfast as the christull,
Firme as the adamant, true as steele,
Immaculate as the sun, without all treason...
He shall be kid conqueror,
For he is kinde lord of al Bretaine that bounds the broad sea.

According to the rest of the prophecy he also becomes king
of Rome, and dies in the Holy Land. (Cf. the gnostic Solovyov's
legend of Antichrist) Commentators identify him with Arthur:
Hic jacet Arturus, rex olim rexque futurus. (See vol. 61 of the
Early English Text Society, 1875)

The Irish call him Hugh. St. Columbkille, Ireland's greatest
prophet pens him thus:

Hugh the magnanimous, the brown-haired, the irresistible,
The smooth-going chariot without blemish,
The subduer of the strangers.

This will be Hugh the undaunted,
To whom the pillars of Tara shall submit.

Students of prophecy who know its Ango-Israel key to the
predictions in the Bible recall that Jeremiah and members of
the royal family of Judah, after being carried captive into
Egypt, escaped and voyaged to Ireland, where the daughter of
Judah's last king, Zedekiah, married the reigning Irish king,
Eocchaid the Heremon. Thence the sceptre of Judah has been
held high from that day to this- fulfilling prophecy - ruling
over the land of Israel. The kings of Ireland became the kings
of Scotland; and when James the Sixth of Scotland became
James the First of England, thereby uniting the two Israel
lands, Jacob's pillow, "the shepherd-stone of Israel," (but known
to the world as the Stone of Scone) became the coronation stone,
beside which all rulers of the Isles (but one) were subsequently
crowned. As for Jeremiah, he became chief judge in an Irish
town which he renamed Tara (from Torah, the law) and tradition relates that he hid the Ark of the Covenant in the mysteri-

ous mound of Tara.

The revealing to the world of the Ark of the Covenant will be *one* of the signs of the latter-day identification as to what lands today represent the Lost Tribes of Israel. Other startling identifications will follow one upon the other until the prophetic fulfillments of Scripture have been witnessed and understood by all.

---

[1] Owen Wister, the American novelist wrote, "We did virtually what we had gone to war with England for doing in 1812. But England did not go to war. She asked for arbitration."

[2] Except in the matter of Ireland.

Don't Pave The Way For Antichrist

A Dialogue between a questioner and interpreter of prophecy.

Questioner: Does Nostradamus say anything about Antichrist?
  Interpreter: He does indeed. A so-far unfulfilled quatrain of his reads:

> The Antichrist three very soon annihilated,
> His war will last seven and twenty years:
> The heretics dead, captives exiled,
> Blood human body, water reddened, hail on earth.

> *L'antechrist trois bien tôt annihilés,*
> *Vingt et sept ans sang durera sa guerre:*
> *Les Hérétiques morts, captifs exilés,*
> *Sang corps humain eau rougie grêler terre.(8.77)*

He probably holds a theology, for his followers are referred to as heretics.

Q: If he is number three, who are the first two?
  I: Actually I do not know, but Hitler would qualify more than satisfactorily as one of them. Friedrich Nietzsche *might* be the other. He called himself the Antichrist and labelled Christianity a dirty religion. If you have read my interpretation of the St. Odile Prophecy you will know enough about these two Antichrists.
Q: How would you define Antichrist?
  I: The Americana definition is as good as any. It reads:

> Antichrist: a term used in the Bible to refer to an evil ruler of power expected to appear at the end of the ages to oppress the Jews or all mankind just before the Day of Judgment.

Q: That sounds like Hitler.

I: I agree. Nevertheless it may describe a tyrant still to come.

Q: I hope not. But haven't you been saying in your lectures that no prophesied future evil is inevitable?

I: You have brought me up short, and I thank you for it. Yes. "Whether there be prophecies, they shall fail." So you and I should pray against the fulfillment of this type of prophecy, and so should mankind. "More things are wrought by prayer than this world dreams of." Let us quote these negative prophecies, yes, but let us quote them to nullify them by earnest affirmations of their opposite.

Only by dedicated and understanding affirmative prayer which insists on the allness of God, the all-good ever-operative and ever-present power, can the world be saved. But first the prayerful within and without the churches must get the evil of gnosticism out of their systems. The Great Apostasy is the modern religionists' unthinking acceptance of the reality of evil, and of matter, as did the ancient gnostics.

Q: Matter and evil look pretty real to me. Does that make me a gnostic?

I: If it becomes warp and woof of your theology.

Q: I have none. I go by common-sense.

I: So did they. Their reasoning was simple: Evil and matter are obviously real, and since God made everything He must have made *them*. Yes, without him was not anything made that was made. Therefore he made such things as smallpox, cancer, murder, tyranny, wars, and indeed all conceivable calamities.

Q: What a hideous theology!

I: Yes, and today this gnosticism is rampant — empatically among the fundamentalists. Gnosticism asserts two contending powers in the universe, both real — not *one* omnipotent power. A gnostic is a dualist.

Acceptance of the reality of evil — a belief rejected with horror by the Church Fathers — paves the way for the reality of Antichrist. But if we are to affirm in prayer the ever-presence of the Kingdom of Heaven, we must conversely unsee any reality in an Antichrist, past, present or future.

Also, we must stop giving aid and comfort to the many petty Antichrists with their hideous kingdoms.

Q: How are we doing that?

I: We — the U. S. A. — good old Uncle Sam — our administration, is propping up little evil empires throughout the world. There are too many of these to talk about. I shall limit myself to signalizing one, about which I know a fair amount — the Central American country named *The Saviour*.

Q: El Salvador?

I: It bears a curious resemblance—withal on a Lilliput scale—to Antichrist Hitler's regime. Let me start from a springboard by quoting Roberto D'Aubuisson, the power sometimes on and sometimes behind the throne in El Salvador, This was a front-page story in some of our newspapers. He was on television in 1982, as government spokesman greeting three German newsmen, and apparently he thought he was flattering them when he said commendingly:

> You Germans are very intelligent; you realized that the Jews were responsible for the spread of communism and you began to kill them.

Q: You're telling me he said that on the air! Wasn't he yanked off the program?

I: No! Why should he be? *He was the representative of his government*. He was not in opposition to it. In El Salvador the Jews are hated only less than the Jesuits. Too bad! If only that brilliant man could be converted from Saul to Paul and then do enough good to more than make up for the evil!

Q: Are you telling me, then, that we are giving military and other help to a government so evil that it openly admires Hitler as some sort of Ideal? I can hardly believe this. Isn't it possible, that all this admiration, ugly though it is, is nothing more than words?

I: No. It is said that imitation is the sincerest form of flattery.

Q: How does El Salvador imitate the Nazi government?

I: The German Antichrist murdered six million Jews of his own and other conquered lands.

Q: I know. Damnable!

I: These were unarmed civilians.

Q: I know.

I: The government we are supporting is also murdering its own citizens, the vast majority of whom were unarmed. it still does it. So far, over 40,000 have been murdered, and half a million of its people have fled the country. In a nation with a total population of under five million, such a number of deaths is a holocaust. And according to the statistics of the International Red Cross 200,000 of its citizens have been displaced.

Q: How does that happen to them?

I: A passing news item in the Christian Science Monitor is revealing. El Salvador needed a dam, which was built, But in so doing it displaced 15,000 peasants. They expected compensation.

Q: Of course.

I: But when the peasants asked the government for their compensation, they were told: "Go away! Get lost!" And when they protested they were called communists, and sometimes shot.

Q: Good God! That's the way to *breed* communism.

I: The best way. No *need* to import it from another country when you can manufacture your own so easily! Suppose, for instance, you were one of these displaced peasants, with a wife and children to support. Your little plot of land has been taken away from you by a sneering government and now you and your family have no place to sleep and whatever job you may have had is lost. At this juncture a friendly fellow from a left-wing organization comes to you with: "We will help you and your family find food, clothing and shelter!" Would you not lean in his direction?

Q: Of course I would. Anyway, I'd have no choice.

I: So all of a sudden you are a communist. At least you now would be, to the government. And your life, and that of your family might well be in jeopardy.

So I say, warningly, helping such a godless regime paves the way for Antichrist, "the man of sin" prophesied in Spripture, or the being Nostradamus calls:

Enemy of the entire human race.

Q: I know. I know. But the argument for siding with evil is, I suppose, balance of power. It seems as though we do have to take sides, and we can't side with Nicaragua, which is the other extreme.

I: It is not. Oh yes, I know that our Secretary of State has pointed an accusing finger at Nicaragua and said, "You are harassing your priests." And our President adds his voice to say to that little country: "You have deported ten priests. How wicked of you!"

Q: Well, isn't that true?

I: Indeed it is. But neither of our two worthies follows up with some sort of balance by pointing the same adminstration finger at El Salvador and saying:

> You are murdering your priests. You have already murdered ten of them, plus a seminarian. And sixty priests have fled the country.

Q: We don't say that?

I: No, we want these murderers on our side, so we must not offend them.

Q: Well! *Real-politik!*

I: It is indeed. Harassment of priests in Nicaragua is *denounced* but there is a strange silence when priests in El Salvador are *murdered*, a strange silence from both our adminstration and our religious leaders and television men of God. It seems to mean then that harassment is a crime much worse than murder. The former is denounced, the latter not![1]

But morality and honor in governments gives way to expediency. The other noon I phoned in to a Los Angeles radio news commentator's talk-show. I referred to horrors perpetrated by the Salvador and Guatamala governments and quoted the Archbishop of San Salvador, who admitted "The trouble is that the people running the country are also running the death squads."

He brushed off the horrors. "These crimes take place," he admitted. "But top priority must be national security, *not* human rights." I was reminded of Roosevelt's quip on Nicaragua's Somoza: "Sure, he's an S.O.B., but he's *our* S.O.B."

Q: How did you respond?

I: I replied: "There is no longer such a thing as national security. All we can do is succeed in wiping out the enemy while he succeeds in wiping *us* out. In a few short years the Khomeinis and the D'Aubuissons of this world will have the atom bomb. So will the Khdafis and the I.R.A. And so may even disgruntled private persons, and assorted ambitious terrorists desirous of ruling the world. Soon there may be a bomb carriable in a suitcase and capable of blowing up a city. And there are those who simmer with an all-encompassing and suicidal hate for others and themselves.

"Our one and only hope on this earth," I concluded, "is prayer." And with prayer, turning from our wicked ways that we may live. There is no such thing on earth as national security. There was. There is, no more. O for that spiritual understanding of God's allness and His all-encompassing protection. We have all forgotten that God is literally — not figuratively— *omnipotent*. We must become gods, like the prophets of old. We must possess the power they possessed and which Jesus demonstrated with the finality of his sonship. Unless we can hold the hand of Omnipotence to the point where we can walk on the ocean or part it, multiply loaves and fishes and say to a mountain, "Be ye removed and be ye cast into the sea," unless we can be superior even to fiery furnace and to the overcoming of death in any shape we are inevitably doomed.

A clue to conquest, though, is a statement by Mrs. Eddy: "Atomic action is Mind, not matter." And John the Revelator prophesies:

The Powers Of Heaven Shall Be Shaken

Say it again, but with one word left in the original Greek:

The Powers Of Ourania Shall Be Shaken

That is the root-word for *uranium*.

If we *understand* that "atomic action is Mind, not matter" and put on the mind of Christ we can defuse all the atom bombs on earth. God *is* omnipotent, and when we see through the veil that covers the nations the Kingdom of Heaven will be found to be *right here*, within us and among us. Our Father made His Kingdom for every one of us, and its coming is inevitable.

Q: I see you put God above even the prophecies of Nostradamus and of the Bible itself.

I: I do. And I have told you why. The men of God of old did this. They have told us we have a free choice between good and evil, and if we hold to the one, we cancel the other.

Q: I have noticed that in your book you have quoted a certain bleak prophecy of Nostradamus which you say sounds like a possible aftermath to atomic fall-out.

I: I have it here. It reads:
The great famine that I sense approaching,
Often turning, then to be universal,
So great and long that one will tear
The root from the wood and the child from the breast.

La grand famine que je sens approcher,
Souvent tourner, puis estre universelle,
Si grande et longue, qu'on viendra arracher
Du bois racine, et l'enfant de mamelle. (1.67)

But I am convinced that any prediction of a woe to come can be converted into a weapon against itself, by utilizing the ever present power of prayer. Specific woes allow for specific and pin-pointed affirmations of their opposite. "Whether there be prophecies, they shall fail." They shall, if we recognize only good as the reality. We are exhorted by the supreme authority on prayer to affirm the present reality of whatever it is we pray for.

Q: Would you apply this perfection-seeing to even the D'Aubuissons and Khomeinis of the world?

I: Yes.

Q: Then D'Aubuisson is a child of God?

I: Even he. I was pleased recently to read in one of Hal Lindsey's books on prophecy that "The real you is perfect." True, so true. So "the real you" of the person, whether he be a Hitler, a Khadafy or a D'Aubuisson is a perfect child of God.

Q: That kind of prayerful thought I would find quite difficult to affirm.

I: Nevertheless, Scripture tells us to do it. Also, any attempt to correct a thought is a move in the right direction.

For instance, many of us need to correct the bruited falsity that the Salvador government is fighting communism. We choose to fancy so because ninety percent of its land is owned by under five percent of its citizens.

As for our administration, it is *not* against communism.

Q: Oh yes it is.

I: If it were it would not palsy up to Red China, with its population of one billion eight-hundred million communists as against six hundred and twenty-eight million Russian reds. And we are arming three Marxist governments.

Q: That's true. That does seem to prove we are not anti-communist, just anti-Russian. But at least the Chinese are not expansionist. They are a peace-loving people.

I: Yes, they are. And a wonderful people. But it may still be a mistake to give them atomic hardware and secrets. Their present generation is peaceful. But look ahead. The 1999 quatrain of Nostradamus may refer to an Asiatic world-conqueror.

Q: How does the prophecy read?

I:
The year 1999 seventh month,
A great king of frightfulness will come from the skies.
To resuscitate the great king of Angolmois;
Around this time Mars will reign for the good cause.

L'an mil neuf cent nonante neuf sept mois,
Du ciel viendra un grand roi d'effrayeur,
Ressusciter le grand roi d'Angolmois;
Avant, apres, regner Mars par bonheur. (10.72)

Q: It sounds as though someone is using Mars as a base to attack earth!

I: I believe so. Notice how much of the quatrain makes sense, even before you try to interpret it. For instance, had the prophecy been dated 1899, 1799, 1699, or 1599, all future dates for Nostradamus, it would have made no sense. Now it begins to.

Q: Who is the great king of frightfulness?

I: I don't know. But he sounds like an Antichrist. I still hold to the view, though, that the "great" Antichrist is an Arab.

Q: What does it mean: great king of Angolmois?

I: Angolmois is an old name for a province of France, so that area will be featured, for some reason. But Edgar Leoni, in interpreting this prophecy, has a very interesting thought, and it may be right. He observes that Angolmois may be an anagram for Mongolois, which would then mean the great Mongol king. In Nostradamus' time, anagrams were popular, and he sometimes used them. According to rules of anagram a one-letter change was allowable, and a one-letter change in this anagram would give you Mongolois. Then *to resuscitate the great Mongol King* would indicate this outer-space character could be a "rescurrected" Ghenghis Khan, a Mongolian Hitler.

Q: And the last line?

I: I believe that Mars means both the planet and the God of War. "For the good cause" would indicate victory pending for the right.

Q: All of this, then, would mean that the next generation of Chinese communists may be of a very different frame of mind from the present generation.

I: Yes. And I am not alone in seeing unwisdom in giving even *good* Chinese atomic secrets. And what about Pakistan, and from thence Khadafy?

Q: Do any other prophets besides Nostradamus say anything about a coming Asiatic conqueror?

I: Yes. One writer on the East says:

It is more than probable that the white race will be obliged to reckon with the influence of the now only legendary king of the world.

And Homer Lea, in his Vermilion Pencil (1908) cites the following Chinese prophecy:

The hour of rebellion is not yet, but will come with a manifestation from heaven, this may be a red star in the east, or when the five flags rise of their own accord from the earth, but more probably when the phoenix sings from the wutang. For at that hour the *man* will have been born, and on that day from all the fields of the empire shall rise up those sown of the dragon's teeth: Then will the silence of the ages be broken, labyrinths uncoil, and a murmur come from depths so deep and unknown that even the world itself shall shrink with dread.

Would this be the one Nostradamus calls "Ver.serp.", that

is, "the true serpent"? I know not.

Q: So we are really not opposed to communism. It's hogwash!

I: Power politics is opposed to everything and to nothing. We cry out against communism to explain an otherwise embarrassing feeling of a need to support a government in our hemisphere so evil it would quickly collapse without our helping hands. A government whose men of might can flaunt arm-band swastikas without serious rebuke. The crooked cross makes of itself a champion against communism. Antichrist Hitler boasted he was a bulwark against that absurd social system. But remember, he also called the Bible "a Bolshevik book" and espoused the Antichrist theology of Nietzsche, espoused it as openly as did Antichrist Nietzsche himself.

Similarly, we support to the hilt a raging tiger of a government (honest, though!) whose D'Aubuisson founds a *Union de Guerreros Blancos*, or Union of White Warriors, with death squads that have openly acknowledged responsibility for many killings that[2] "Incensed by the Jesuit order's advocacy of agrarian reforms, in 1977., the I.U.G.B. threatened to kill all Jesuits remaining in El Salvador after a certain date." After that date it promised open season on priests, and to date ten priests have been assassinated. Its death squads even handed out flyers urging:

Serve Your Country. Kill A Priest!

Q: If we know all this we are certainly paving the way for Antichrist.

I: We do know this. But mention these facts to some people and their eyes glaze. We are indeed supporting this and other Lilliput empires of evil. *Schrechlichkeit*, or Frightfulness. It wants its "retributive" murders to be known: therefore they are melodramatically performed in public. The greatly loved Archbishop Oscar Romero is shot in front of his congregation as he elevates the host. The gunman coolly pockets his gun with silencer, stands up and walks out through the congregation. "See," the Antichrist government in essence jeers: "better watch out, or this will happen to you." Atilio Ramirez Amaya, the judge put in charge of the investigation is himself the victim of an assassination attempt, and he flees the country with his family.

A Sunday School teacher explaining Scripture to his young students is shot, with them! And so are a surgeon and the patient he is operating on. Four of our American church-women are roadblocked, raped and murdered by five National Guardsmen who explain - apparently truthfully — that they are only obeying orders. Four Dutch television newspapermen are butchered, and a Newsweek photographer. (Apparently it is open season on gentlemen of the press) According to Duarte 32 mayors (actually 60, by now) 5 top party union officials and 600 party members have been murdered. D'Aubuisson goes on television to denounce his attorney general Mario Zamora as a communist.[3] Five days later Zamora "is giving a party when gunmen burst into his living room on the night of February 23, 1980." He identifies himself quickly to the intruders so his guests won't be mown down with him. He is then dragged into the bathroom and shot through the head. Another time D'Aubuisson goes on the air to denounce Reagan's meddling in Salvadoran affairs in sending over two land reform advisors to assist Roberto Viera, head of the Salvador Land Reform Institution. Two and a half weeks later all three are murdered in the Hotel Sheraton Coffee Shop. And neither government seems to care!

Dead bodies of unarmed civilians are thrown into body dumps, or into the streets, often mutilated: that is, without an eye, a penis, a hand, an ear, a nose, etc. Sometimes the bodies are placed on bus benches, in a sitting position, as if waiting for a bus. Or in rest rooms, on toilet seats.[4]

A typical example of mutilation is that of one of our Americans. John Sullivan, reporter disappeared from the San Salvador Hotel on December 28, 1980. His family placed ads in a local newspaper. Five months later a brave Salvadoran[5] told them where the body of an American had been buried. A stick of dynamite had apparently been detonated. Then his hands were cut off. So no fingerprints. But the pavers of the way for Antichrist were not quite smart enough. "In February 1983 the body was identified by U.S. pathologists as Sullivan's".[6]

Q: And who carried out the murders?

I: Well, "local officials supervised by security forces buried the body." Apparently all was quiet and peaceful until the body was found, But so far, nobody is blameworthy, according to this antichrist government, which our Secretary of State assures us is "pro-American."

Q: I don't understand. This is the government *we are giving arms to?* And they murder our citizens?

I: With enthusiasm. At least eight, so far.

Q: And you say our Secretary of State calls El Salvador "pro-American?"

I: He does indeed. But, as the saying goes, "With such friends, who needs enemies?"

Now, let me indulge in a prophecy. It is not a psychic nor inspirational prophecy. It is based on my average man understanding of the laws of our Creator. I believe that we are under the judgment of God for our support of a wicked and even satanic regime, which treats us with continuing contempt, which sneers at us the more we unconditionally help it. When Queen Elizabeth the First learned that one of her English subjects had been mistreated and was in a French prison, she sent her seamen to rescue him. But we don't even dare say, please, sirs, don't murder any more of our nuns. Please don't torture and decapitate any more of our newsmen. I am trying to stand tall and you are not helping our image. Please don't assassinate any more of our land reform experts. We are sending you only good men. And we are sending them only that they might help you. We are not exporting communism to you. Remember, we are sending you guns. But please, please don't murder our citizens. If you do that any more I shall be forced to say "Fie on you!"

Q: But isn't it a little better under the presidency of Duarte? He was tortured himself, you know. He stood for principle. He's a Christian Democrat.

I: He neither rules nor governs. There is one party: the militia. The military is the absolute lord. And to the military a Christian Democrat is a communist. The one-party press calls Duarte a communist. Antichrist is still petty king in El Salvador. And we are paving the way for more and ever more villainy. Satan has not changed his habits.

Q: Even since the election?

I: Even since the election. A prominent conservative newpaper columnist has been shot to death and ditto a computer operator whose statistics were not palatable. And we still deport refugees back to the frightful home they fled, at the rate of a little under a thousand a month. And they are still being murdered when they get back. The wickedness is like that of sending Jews back to Nazi Germany. I happen to know, because I have given concert benefits for the refugees, and I hear with a reasonably accurate ear the tragic stories of what happens to these poor people. The numbers of the innocents sent back are smaller, but their deaths are undoubted The Archbishop of San Salvador has estimated that "35% of these deportees lose their lives within six months of returning to El Salvador." Some are murdered on arrival.

The army massacred sixty-eight civilians in eight small villages as recently as mid-July of 1984. The human Rights office of the Roman Catholic Church has compiled more than forty photographs of the murdered. "Most of those who were killed," states the director, "were children, women, and elderly people." Some were tortured and physically mutilated, and some of the women were raped before being killed. The army likes to have its fun! The photos are gruesome, hideous.

Our Leader waves the Bible about. But he should open it. To El Salvador and some of the other nations he is helping he should read aloud from the prophet Micah:

Woe to them that devise inequity, and work evil upon their beds! When the morning is light, they practise it, because it is in the power of their hand.
And they covet fields, and take them by violence; and houses, and take them away: so they oppress a man and his house, even a man and his heritage.

---

[1] But there is again a Real-politik reason: Our president was upset when Panama was given back the administration of her own canal. But if we mine Nicaraguan waters and wage war with that little land we can take it over and carve out of it a fine canal for ourselves!

And the iniquity of Nicaragua building an air field when we have only twelve of our own in Honduras!

[2] According to Current Biography, 1983, under D'Aubuisson.

[3] Easy to do, by D'Aubuisson definition. He said to an L.A. Times reporter in

El Salvador: "You can be a communist even it you personally don't believe you are a communist." (12/18/83)

[4] In his first speech since arriving in El Salvador in September, 1983 Ambassador Pickering stated to the American Chamber of Commerce, "What has distressed my government is the lack of action against those who murder and kidnap university professors, doctors, labor leaders, campesinos and government workers...No one wants to live in a country where no efforts are made to find who dumps bodies in gas stations and parking lots....Where are the condemnations? Why hasn't the private sector condemned such outrages? Why haven't the daily papers done so?" (Santa Ana Register, Nov. 26/83)

[5] An article in the Christian Science Monitor is revealingly headed: "Salvadorans See and Hear 'Nothing' when Neighbors Disappear."

[6] Associated Press (5/22/84).

Armageddon!

The following chapter, which is mainly an interpretation of certain prophecies of Nostradamus on the final war of all, first appeared years ago in a book-magazine entitled *What the Future Holds*. In my opinion this prophetic article is remarkable, not only in itself, but because of the time when it was published; and for the latter reason it is re-printed here. As a prophecy, "Armageddon" has not begun to date, and today it is even more easily understood than when it was first published.

The reader will observe that "Armageddon" concerns a mighty Arab empire. He will also observe that mention is made of "the Arab League." In 1942, when this article was originally published, there was no mighty Arab empire and no Arab league. Now there is an Arab league and the mighty Arab empire is *beginning* to be.

The Prophecy

Armageddon has not yet come. Armageddon is the war which will end war and usher in the "millennium." The name is derived from Megiddo, a plain in Palestine, and the Bible says the culminating battle is to be fought there. Probably the entire war will be over the Holy Land. It will be a religious war.

Many students of Bible prophecy thought the first World War would be Armageddon. Many of them thought World War Two was Armageddon. They were wrong. Both the Bible and Nostradamus (to say nothing of other prophets) agree that the great pre- millennial war is to take place in the future—though in this century—and that it will be a war between East and West, with the Arabian people as the "villain" and the other races of the East united under a conquering Arab Prince.

For centuries many Bible students have been aware that the final time of trouble would be with Edom (the Arabs). Mede, Lowch, Newton and Faber, who wrote about 150 years ago, agreed that "the fall of Edom was to be the rise of the house of Israel."

Dr. Grattan Guiness, student of Bible prophecy, made this warning prediction in 1878:

> We have noted various indications in the conditions of Palestine and of Israel, and in the political events of our own day, which seem to indicate that the cleansing of the sanctuary and the restoration of Israel are not distant.
>
> When these shall take place, when the Moslems, now driven out of Bulgaria, shall be driven also out of Syria, when the nations of Europe, actuated it may be by mutual distrust and political jealousy, or it may be by higher motives, shall conspire to reinstate the Jews in the land of their forefathers, then the last warning bell will have rung; then the last of the unfulfilled predictions of Scriptures as to events prior to the great crisis, will have received its accomplishment; then the second advent of Israel's rejected Messiah to reign in conjunction with His glorified saints as King over all the earth, will be close at hand; then the mystery of God will be all but finished, and the manifestation of Christ immediate . . . The destruction of the power and independence of the Ottoman Empire should be as a trumpet blast to Christendom proclaiming that the day of Christ is at hand.

An Anglo-Israelite, A. B. Traina, interprets Armageddon even more pointedly. In a little circular published a few years ago he wrote:

The Final Act In the Drama
(Still Future)

The history of the quarrel between Judah and Edom is recounted by the prophet Obadiah, chapter 1, verses 1-14. The sequel still to be fulfilled is recounted in the latter part of the chapter. The chief characters of the drama still to be unrolled before the eyes of the world, with the Holy Land as the scene, are Edom (the Arabs), Judah (the Jews), and Ephraim (England). Edom is the villain, Judah the victim, and Ephraim the hero who rescues the victim, and in the end there is peace forevermore.

The final world problem, then will concern the re-establish-ment of Judah in Zion.

The War Of Religions

In the war of Armageddon the Jews will play collectively the biggest part they will ever have played in history. Zechariah writes: "It shall come to pass in that day, that a great tumult from the Lord shall be among them. . . . And Judah *also* shall fight at Jerusalem." (14:13,14)

Nostradamus, like the Bible prophets, knew that Armageddon is still to come. He knew Armageddon was not simply a general war in which the final battle would happen to be fought in the Holy Land. He knew, as the Bible prophets knew, that this war would be a war between Infidel and Christian, as in the old days of the Crusades. Indeed, he calls the opponents of the Arab Prince "les croisés," "the Crusaders." Palestine is to be the pivotal point of the whole war and of its clashing ideologies.

Nostradamus calls the conqueror "the true serpent." John on Patmos calls him "the false prophet," and "the lamb with two horns." For centuries interpreters of the Apocalypse have understood these two designations as references to Mohammed. The great Prophet of Allah himself agreed that he was accurately symbolized as "Dhul Qarnain," or "the two-horned one" (see Koran, Chapter 18). The crescent moon is the emblem of Mohammedan power.

St. Odile writes that at the end of the Hitler war, "the two horns of the moon will be united to the cross," meaning that Turkey (in this case) will be on the same side of the fence as the Allies. But not in Armageddon! So obvious is this interpretation that is has been accepted by most students of Bible prophecy, while Howard Rand, in his *Study in Revelation* writes, "The false prophet is easily identified as Mohammed, whose followers adopted the emblem of the crescent moon and the star."

The Apocalyptic Number 666

Of this "false prophet"[1] John further says, "Let the discerning calculate the cipher of the Beast; it is the cipher of a man, and the figures are six hundred and sixty-six."

The number has been applied by wishful thinkers to every "beast" from Nero to Hitler. Take Der Fuehrer for instance: if the letter A is given the numerical value of 100; B 101, and so on, the six letters of his name will total 666, which is curious and interesting.

The trouble is that the numerical values are arbitrary, and not those employed by John. But a man who can read Revelation in the original Greek has informed me that Mohammed meets the numerical qualifications. This is borne out by James Winthrop, a noted Bible scholar, who wrote in 1809, "The name, mark or number of a name, is a distinction adopted by the Beast and his image, and by the Mohometans."

The actual *founder* of Islam, who was a good man, is not meant by these designations. They apply to an apparent *follower* of his, who is to appear in the latter days. John states that he will be a great magician—that is a worker of wonders, an emulator of Jesus:

> He doeth great wonders, so that he maketh fire come down from heaven on the earth in the sight of men. And he deceiveth them that dwell on the earth by the means of those miracles which he had power to do in the sight of the (first)beast.

This tallies with Nostradamus' statement that he will be "of the league of the great Hermes," and possess "a magic wand." He will understand that all things are thoughts and therefore subject to the control of him who is aware of that simple fact.

First Triumphs Of The Arab Conqueror

This power "to bring down lightning from heaven" and control the forces of nature will enable him to rally millions to him. He will proclaim himself the Messiah and set out to reform the earth and establish universal peace. By waging war!

> The Arab prince Mars, Sun, Venus, Leo
> Reign of the Church will succumb by sea:
> Towards Persia nearly a million,
> The true serpent will invade Constantinople and Egypt.

(5.25)

To the devout Nostradamus "the Church" is always the

Catholic Church. The second line of the prophecy describes the fate of one of the Popes.

"The Vile Person"

The Arab Conqueror will not only cause the Catholic Church to crash (temporarily), but will also invade the Holy Land. This explains why "Judah will fight at Jerusalem." Since the Conqueror who invades Egypt is also to take Libya—as Nostradamus writes elsewhere—he is probably "the vile person" who, according to Daniel, is to arise "in the time of the end."

> He shall also invade the fair land of Palestine, and myriads shall be killed. . . . As he exerts his force against the various lands, the land of Egypt shall not escape, but he shall lay hands on the treasures of gold and silver and all the valuables in Egypt, the Libyans and the Ethiopians following in his train.
>
> Then rumors from the east and the north shall alarm him, till he retires in great fury to inflict doom and destruction on many, pitching his royal pavilions between the Mediterranean and the sacred hill so fair. . . and there shall be a time of trouble such as never has been since there was nation. . . . And now, Daniel, keep all this a close secret and keep the book shut as a secret, till the crisis at the end; here then many shall give way and trouble shall be multiplied on earth. (Chapters 11 and 12)

In his Epistle to Henry the Second, Nostradamus tells of these times:

> A new incursion shall be made from the maritime shores (England and America), eager to give the leap of liberty since the first taking by the Mahometans. Their assaults shall not be at all in vain, and in the place where the habitation of Abraham was, it shall be assailed by those who hold the Jovialists in reverence. . . . The Holy Sepulcher, for so long a period and object of great veneration, shall remain exposed to the blighting dew of evening under the stars of heaven, and of the sun and moon. The holy place (Bethlehem) shall be converted into a stable for cattle small and large, and applied to other base purposes . . . ."

In quatrain 90 of Century 8 the prophet doubtless refers to the same military occupation:

When among the Crusaders one is found of troubled mind,
A horned ox will be seen in the Holy Land,

Then the home of the Virgin will be filled with swine.
The King will no longer be able to sustain order there.

(8.90)

The horned ox, like the horned lamb in Revelation, represents the power of Islam.

The Arab Prince To Invade Europe

Backed now by "the forces of Asia,," the conqueror from Tartary will invade Europe:

Libyan Prince Powerful in the Occident,
He will come from Araby . . .

But he will not behave like a Christian:

From Fez the reign will come to those of Europe,
Fire to their city, and blade will slash:
The great Lord of Asia, land and sea with great troop,
So that he will pursue to the death blues, fathers, the cross.

France may be the first of his conquests:

Because of the discord and negligence of the French,
A passage will be opened to Mahomet . . .

He will have a mighty air force, and will probably attack in the white season:

The Oriental[1] will leave his seat,
He will pass the Appenine mountains, to see France;
He will pierce through the sky, the waters and snow,
And he will strike everyone with his rod.

The British will thoughtfully move the seat of their government to this continent to escape the Oriental's air blitzes:

In the very deepest part of the English Occident
Where the head of the British Isle will be . . .

But Nostradamus' beloved France will be less fortunate. The "true serpent" will destroy Paris with his air fleet:

Live fire will be left, hidden death,
Within the globes, horrible, frightful.
By night a fleet will reduce the city to rubble.
The city on fire, the enemy indulgent.

After his conquest of France he will introduce culture:

Learned in letters, he will be condescending,
And have the Arabian language translated into French.

And he will introduce his culture into Italy too:

The African heart will come from the Orient,
To vex Adria and the Heirs of Romulus,
Accompanied by the Libyan fleet,
Malta will tremble and neighboring isles empty.

At Naples, Palermo, Sicily, Syracuse,
New tyrants, lightnings, fires in the skies. . . .

Naples, Palermo, and all Sicily,
Will be inhabited by the barbarian hand. . . .

The French prophet only once uses the expression "barbarian" for German, otherwise for Mohammedan.

He is to "strike *everyone* with his rod," so all nations will be involved. Even neutral Switzerland:

Migrate, migrate from Geneva all of you:
Saturn of gold will change to iron.
The one against Raypoz will exterminate all.
Before the event there will be signs in the heavens.

He will sweep into Germany:

In the Rhine and in the Danube the great Camel will come to drink, and will not regret it . . .

Germany's ancient enemies will be on the side of the invaders:

The Church of God, will be persecuted
And the holy temples will be despoiled:
The child will reduce the mother to nakedness in chemise,
The Arabs will rally to the Poles.

Turning Of The Tide

But at this point the Christian and democratic powers will begin to wake up:

A Germanic heart will be born of Trojan blood,
Who will attain to very high power:
He will drive out the foreign Arabian people,
Restoring the Church to its pristine pre-eminence.

The conqueror will be undermined at his seat of government— which he had taken by force:

The great Arab will march well ahead,
But he will be betrayed by those of Constantinople . . .
We will help "give the leap of liberty":

The people of Rhodes will demand aid,
Abandoned by the neglect of their heirs,
The Arab empire will re-evaluate its course,
The cause redressed by the Hesperians.

Note that last line: "Hesperians" is frequently used by Nostradamus to mean the people of the land over the sea, west of France, the land where the golden apples grow. So America will help save the day.

Part of the following quatrain seems to look ahead to the state of things *after* Armageddon:

Cross, peace, under an accomplished divine word
Spain and France will be united together,
Great calamity near, and very bitter combat,
No heart so stoute that it will not tremble.

A long-awaited French ruler will also help to overcome the conqueror:

The frizzled black beard by engines
Will subjugate the cruel, proud people:
A great Chyren will take from captivity
All the prisoners under Mohammed's banner.

"Chyren" has been understood as an anagram of "Henryc" (a French King) ever since Nostradamus penned this prophecy.

Great Ogmion will approach Constantinople,
The barbaric league will be driven out...

"Ogmion" or "Ogmius" is the French Hercules, according to Larousse.

How Armageddon Will End

Now let the Bible take up the story — though Nostradamus has written much more on the man. According to most interpreters of the book of Revelation, the river Euphrates symbolizes the Ottoman Empire. At this time, the book says, the Euphrates is to dry up. That is interpreted as symbolizing the end of the Ottoman power. Remember that Nostradamus has already explained that the Arab prince rules from captured Constantinople.

The terrific "battle of the great day of God Almighty" takes place on the plains of Armageddon. "And the seventh angel poured out his vial into the air; and there came a great voice out of the temple of heaven, from the throne, saying, It is finished."

The close of Armageddon is accompanied by great upheavals of nature. John on Patmos writes:

> And there were voices, and thunders, and lightnings; and there was a great earthquake, such as was not since men were upon the earth; so mighty an earthquake and so great.... And the cities of the nations fell...and every island fled away, and the mountains were not found.
>
> (Chapter 16)

While Nostradamus writes:

> There will be in the month of October a great translation made, such that one would think that the librating body of the earth had lost its natural movement in the abyss of perpetual darkness. There will be seen precursive signs in the springtime, and after extreme changes ensuing, reversal of kingdoms, and great earthquakes. . . Then by great deluges the memory of things will suffer incalculable loss.

The prophet Obadiah adds his confirmatory voice:

> Yes, the day of the Eternal is at hand, with doom for all the nations. You on my sacred hill have drunk the cup, and so shall every nation drink it at my hand, drink it and stagger and vanish.
>
> But your survivors shall hold Zion hill, and it shall be inviolate; the house of Jacob shall regain their heritage. For the house

of Jacob (all Israel) shall be fire (mighty in war), and Joseph's house (England and America) a flame, with Esau's house (forces of Asia) as straw to be kindled and consumed, till not a soul is left of Esau's house—by order of the eternal . . .

The Holy Land Is Free Again

The prophet Isaiah rejoices with exceeding great joy at the outcome of the great war:

Awake, awake; put on thy strength, O Zion; put on thy beautiful garments, O Jerusalem, the holy city: for henceforth there shall no more come into thee the unclean. Shake thyself from the dust; arise and sit down, O Jerusalem: loose thyself, O captive daughter of Zion. . . How beautiful upon the mountains are the feet of him that bringeth good tidings, that publisheth peace . . . that saith unto Zion, Thy God reigneth! Thy watchmen (those who have held the mandate) shall lift up the voice; with the voice together shall they sing; for they shall see eye to eye, when the Lord shall bring again Zion. Break forth into joy, sing together ye waste places of Jerusalem; for the Lord hath comforted his people, he hath redeemed Jerusalem.

The Lord hath made bare his holy arm in the eyes of all the nations: and all the ends of the earth shall see the salvation of our God."

Nostradamus, too, has his say on this inspiring victory of the Cross over the crescent moon. And the last line of the following prophecy is a stunning example of an irony that is typically French:

The new law to occupy the new land,
Towards Syria, Judea and Palestine,
The great barbarian Empire will fail down
Before the moon completes her cycle.

---

[1] It will be observed that I left the "false prophet" in quotation marks, as I do not hold that opinion. Mohammed brought his followers to the belief in one indivisible God, and accepted both the Virgin birth of Jesus and His Resurrection. He was an authentic prophet.

[1] The man from the East. Not the Far East, which to Nostradamus is Asia.

The New Order

In the ages to come, materialism will cease, sickness will disappear and about 2000 A.D. will see "the end of evils begun." Even death will be overcome.

The first verse of an inspiring hymn for our latter days reads:

God is working His purpose out
As year succeeds to year,
God is working His purpose out
And the time is drawing near;
Nearer and nearer draws the time,
The time that shall surely be,
When the earth shall be filled with the glory of God
As the waters cover the sea.

But before true religion (not Churchianity!) can prevail, materialism and false religion must be swept away. And before the New Order of the Ages can prevail the old order must crumble or crash. An integral part of this old order is what the book of Revelation calls BABYLON; typifying the power that money brings, faith in the omnipotence of lucre, ruthless high finance. The literal Babylon, or money-power, was yet to fall. The inspired Revelator saw its doom:

Another angel shouted aloud with a strong voice, "Fallen, fallen is Babylon the great . . . the kings of the earth have committed vice with her, *and by the wealth of her wantonness earth's traders have grown rich."* . . . she shall be burnt with fire . . . *and the traders of earth shall weep and wail over her; for now there is no one to buy their freights,* freights of gold, silver, jewels, pearls . . . fine flour and wheat, with cattle, sheep, horses, carriages, slaves, *and the souls of men.* The traders in these wares, who made rich profits from her, will stand far off for fear of her torture, weeping and wailing. . . And all shipmasters and seafaring folk, sailors and all whose business lies upon the sea, stood far off as they watched the smoke of her burning, crying, "What city was like the great city?"

Woe and alas for the great city, where all shipment made rich profit by her treasures! . . . The magnates of earth were thy traders: all nations were seduced by thy magic spells. And in her was found the blood of all . . . who were slain upon earth . . .

(Revelation, 18, Moffatt's version).

There is great rejoicing in heaven at her fall: "Hallelujah! And the smoke of her goes up for ever and ever!"

Even our gentle Lord could not bear expressing his loathing and contempt for the lovers of Mammon: "Go to now, ye rich men, weep and howl . . . Ye have heaped treasure together . . Ye have lived in pleasure and been wanton."

Perhaps the American prophet John Ballou Newbrough had an inkling of the truth when (in 1889) he predicted for 1947, "All nations will be demolished and all the earth be thrown open to all people to go and come as they please." He dated this too early, however.

According to the Bible, after Armageddon Jerusalem will become the lighthouse of the ends of the earth. And from this holy city the Anglo-Saxon-Celtic peoples, together with the Jews, will govern the world. Jerusalem will be a new and wiser Geneva, the seat of a great world federation. By this time the Jews will have accepted the Christ, according to Zechariah, who says, "They shall look upon me whom they have pierced (Jesus) and they shall mourn for him as one mourneth for his only son." And in their new-found missionary zeal they will set out to visit the dark places of the earth and spread the Gospel of Christ everywhere. "In those days it shall come to pass that ten men shall take hold, out of all the languages of the nations, even shall take hold of the skirt of him that is a Jew, saying, "We will go with you; for we have heard that God is with you.' "(Zech. 8:23)

The Dead Will Be Raised

The last line of the quatrain describes a wonderful event. We may recall Jesus' prophecy that the time would come when

Christians would perform greater works than the master himself. Here we see that healing power will be so developed in mankind that the dead can be raised in droves at a time.

How will the fulfillment of this prophecy be possible? By following our Lord's affirmative prayer that whatsoever we ask for we already have. There is no time limitation in God's mind. So if we want a dead person to have life we must *know* that person *already* has life.

The Church Fathers knew this so well. Said Theodoret, "It is impossible for the immortal nature to undergo death." And St. Anselm, "Mortality does not belong to the Pure Nature of Man." And St. Athanasius, "Life then does not die, but quickens the dead. " And St. Hilary, "What is divine is not liable to destruction. " And St. Hippolytus, "For the incorruptible nature is not the subject of generation; it grows not, sleeps not, hungers not, thirsts not, is wearied not, suffers not, dies not, it is not pierced by nails and spear, sweats not, drops not with blood."

Affirmed St. Justin's pupil, Tatian, in his Address to the Greeks:

> We were not created to die, but we die by our own fault. Our free will has destroyed us; we who were free have become slaves; we have been sold through sin. Nothing evil has been created by God; we ourselves have manifested wickedness; but we, who have manifested it, are able again to reject it.

Nostradamus was a spiritually-minded man, whose vision pierced through time as easily as the sun's rays pierce through transparent glass. He looked into the future and saw his Grand Monarch; then, in turn, Louis XVI and the French Revolution, Napoleon and his devastating wars, the fall of France in 1870, then World War I.

The great 16th century French prophet similarly saw World War II, with Europe under the heel of "Hister" . . . he saw Franco and named him . . . he saw "a doddering old man head of France, the country divided and conceded to gendarmes. " . . . he saw the doom of Germany . . . followed by a hectic peace. He looks farther and sees the awakening East . . . he sees their Messiah rise, the "true serpent," the Lord of Asia. He sees another mighty invasion of Europe. He looks even farther . . . he sees the barbarian empire crash like thunder, while a new law of righeousness arises in Palestine . . . he sees "the end of evils begun" . . . "the dead will come out of their tombs." He looks farther . . . farther . . . farther . . . until:

> The body without soul will no longer be as a sacrifice
> Day of death will change to day of birth,
> The Divine Spirit will make the soul happy,
> Seeing the Word in its eternity.

Man then will be altogether perfect. He will see God directly, without benefit of the material senses. All things will be under his feet:

> The Divine Word will give to substance,
> Comprising heaven, earth, hidden gold, mystical fact,
> Body, soul, spirit, having all power,
> As much under its feet as in the heavenly seat.

Man, in that distant day, will be like God. He will understand all mysteries. There will be no material substance, for substance "comprises heaven, earth, hidden gold, mystical fact." Man will be the body or embodiment of "soul, spirit," and therefore have "all power" and all knowledge.

Indestructible and eternal, man then will be satisfied, for he will be awake, in His likeness."

Sin, Disease And Death Overcome

Prophets, it is said, are a gloomy lot. They predict troubles, calamities, earthquakes, floods, wars and rumors of wars. They do; but looking farther they also predict the end of these woes. For instance, Nostradamus sees Napoleon and his butcheries. But he sees St. Helena too: "The great man will be carried away in an iron cage to a place that is but a rock." St. Odile sees Hitler and his countless atrocities. But she sees his end. And "the sun will shine with a new and glorious radiance." These evils come, but woe to him by whom they come!

As sin is conquered in individual consciousness, evils of all kinds will proportionately diminish. Sickness will wane and vanish. Old age will disappear and give place to eternal youth. Consciousness of Life will become so powerful as to make death skulk and run. "The last enemy that shall be destroyed is death." It will be destroyed not only in ourselves, but in others.

"And He will destroy in this mountain the face of the covering cast over all people, and the veil that is spread over all nations. He will swallow up death in victory; and the Lord God will wipe away tears from off all faces; and the rebuke of His people shall He take away from off all the earth: for the Lord hath spoken it."

Nostradamus is helpful here: he tells us when these things shall begin to be. Around the year 2000 will be the "end of evils begun," and:

> At the revolution of the great number seven,
> It will happen, in the time of the games of the hecatomb.
> Not far from the great age thousand
> That the dead will arise from their tombs.

According to the Biblical calculations of our seer)which were quite orthodox) the world was almost five thousand years old with the Advent of Christ Jesus. Two thousand years added to that figure gives "the revolution of the great number seven" near "the great age thousand," *i.e.,* the seventh revolution of the year thousand since creation.

Letter From A Higher Critic

May 5, 2415

Mark Livingstone,
25 The Standards,
Verneville, Alassippi

Dear Mark:

In your last letter you made one palpable hit, but only one: I admit that the atomic wars of the Twenty-first Century and the cataclysms of the Twenty-second Century destroyed so much of our cultural inheritance, including nearly all our Nineteenth and Twentieth Century history, that there is very little we can turn to of those times that is authentic. Apparently that is the only point we will be able to agree on.

I cannot possibly believe, for instance, as you do, that there ever did exist an Abraham Lincoln as so glowingly portrayed by our two or three surviving "history" digests; nor can I believe that there ever was a World War II, at least such as they describe. Wars, Yes—there have always been wars, and a World War II may have occurred—but certainly not with such incredible concomitants.

In short, your "history" is much too fictional for me.

So pardon me if I prove my point by doing a hatchet job on this medley of stuff you seem so sure of, this "history" which is about as reliable and as imaginatively romantic as the Bible myths. My method of demolition will be identical to that of those commendably clear-headed iconoclasts of earlier days, the Higher Critics. What they did to the Bible, including the

Moses and Christ legends, I shall do with our nearly equally revered American history, so called, and perhaps more thoroughly.

Let me begin my act of demolition by making an analogy, one that is possible thanks to the fortunate survival of that now famous Lord Chumley collection of Old English plays. In browsing through some of the playwrights of the Elizebethan, Restoration and even later periods I noticed that they had a cute habit of giving names to their characters that fitted the parts they played in the plots. For instance, Sir Giles Overreach was overreaching, Abhorson was a nasty fellow, Sir Fopling Flutter was an effeminate daddy, Wellborn was a fine young gentleman, and so on.

Now it is precisely this fictional method of applying names that dismays me when I see the obvious evidences of it in our so-called American history, and thus I am led to the inescapable conclusion that what so many of us regard as history is not history at all but pure romancing by flag-waving minstrels, though it has come down to us as sober fact. Not that this legend-building is anything new. The Song of Roland and the deeds of Arthur and the Knights of the Grail were all once considered historical. Those romances, with a little history mixed in, were simply the troubadours', skalds' or minstrels' exploitation and exaltation of their respective heroes and lands.

Now let me get down to brass tacks with my higher criticism and start in with "World War II." This terrific conflict, so the story goes, resulted in the victory of right over wrong, of decency over tyranny, of the Anglo-Saxon peoples (mainly) over the wicked Teutons! There was a big bad wolf in this fairytale named Adolph Hitler, a German ogre who burned people alive in ovens by the millions and who nearly conquered the world! Now don't you think that whoever made up this part of the yarn knew that the name Adolph in Old High German means Wolf Prince? And isn't it a coincidence that he descended like a wolf on the fold on the innocent sheep nations of Poland, Czechoslovakia and other helpless countries? This name is a fancy of the poets, surely!

Let us proceed. The great nation France is beaten to its knees by the mighty marauder, whereupon a folk-hero named De Gaulle arises who fights on against all odds, and later, with the coming of peace, assumes rule over a united Gaul. His name was beautifully tailored for his part. note that it means "Of France" or "Of the French," indicating that he was a true patriot, French of the French.

The names of the Russian leaders in this war also indicate the poet's imaginative pen. The Wolf Prince met with real resistance in his invasion of Russia, because the opposition here was headed by Stalin, which means Steel, and his high henchman Molotov, which signifies Hammer.(Probably the names also represented the Hammer and Sickle, symbols of the Communist cause.)

This mythical invasion of Russia by the German tyrant is no doubt simply a furbishing up of the earlier yarn of the invasion of this same land by the equally fabulous Napoleon, that is, Appollyon, the Destroyer, which the name means in Greek. Both conquerors invade with mighty multitudes, and both conquerors are trounced. Justice must triumph!

Now across the Channel, at the outset of the Great War, so the story goes on, The British Empire was ruled by a mere servant- leader, fittingly named Chamberlain. But so desperate did the danger of the Wolf Prince's invasion become that the chamberlain was forced to give way to the Master Defender of the British Isles, Churchill, the Church on the Hill, of course, representing the staunch, unshakable faith of the stubborn bulldog British. This name was clearly chosen for its positive, spiritual sound.

And across the Atlantic, where the Giant Ally of the Church on the Hill was preparing for war, the names of the protagonists were equally descriptive of their functions. As America was one of the *good* nations the names were selected for their affirmative sound. The great wartime President was Roosevelt, which is Dutch for Field of Roses. A name of excellent odor! Fabled to have written the President's wartime and other speeches was Rosenman, that is, the Rose Man, the gardener who takes care of the flowers of speech of the Field of Roses. And the Secretary of the Treasury, the man who had charge of the finances that kept the nation functioning was Morgenthau, symbolizing that he supplied the refreshing morning dew for the roses. And the Secretary of State, that is, the ship of state, was of course good old Hull.

Well, I could go on for our romancing historians enjoyed the creation of such curious coincidences. Here's another obvious one: Just as they had dusted off the Napoleon Apollyon legend to re-apply it to the Wolf prince, so in like manner they borrowed s still earlier so-called historical event, reversed it to disguise the source, and applied it to the Great War. In 1066, so it was fabled and generally believed, Normandy invaded England. At the head of the invading troops, so the minstrels reported, was a minstrel-warrior named Taillefer, a hero who struck the first blow of the war. So our latter-day minstrels fabled that just as Normandy invaded England, England and the Allies now invaded Normandy. And to the leader of the conquering forces the poet historians gave that same name of Taillefer, only this time they translated it first into German, Eisenhower. Both names, you are aware, mean Iron-Hewer, a most fitting epithet for men of war!

Now let me ask a rhetorical question. Do you really believe that these names: Adolph Hitler, De Gaulle, Molotov, Stalin, Chamberlain, Churchill, Roosevelt, Rosenman, Morgenthau, Hull and Eisenhower could have sprung up by chance? And yet if they are real historical names chance and chance alone must have operated in their selection. Therefore, I say that this history, that you and so many others credit as true history, is as legendary as the Bible stories, and for similar reasons. True history is meaningless and springs by happenstance from a meaningless world.

I note that you also mention in your letters, and frequently, that American folk-hero, Abraham Lincoln, and you actually seem to be convinced there was such a man. I, too, should certainly like to be able to believe the human race capable of producing so noble a being, but here is just another instance where the facts firmly forbid me to do so. As usual, let us first analyze the name. Abraham was well-chosen. It immediately suggests. Father Abraham, the Bible patriarch. The name is Hebrew and means Father of a Multitude. All this Lincoln was. He loomed above the Civil War like a colossus, holding the nation together and keeping it one and indivisible. Preserver of the nation, saviour of his people, he was veritably the father figure of a multitude, was he not? And a father figure on which the conspirators could vent their malice.

Notice, too, how so frequently he is likened to the Saviour of Mankind. Ponder that beautiful surviving pen and ink drawing, so well portraying America's conception of a vast, compassionate, Christ-like figure. Ah, that Lincoln! One of the most beautiful creations of our dreaming skalds. Would that I could accept him! Our poet-patriots made up a perfect parallel between him and the solar myth saviour of mankind. As follows:

Christ was a martyr.
Lincoln was a martyr.
Christ was slain on Good Friday.
Lincoln was slain on Good Friday.
So Lincoln joins the crucified saviours of mankind.

Now whatever this story is, it is not history. It could not possibly be. It stands to reason the assassins of Lincoln would not have likened him to the All Good Man, so they could not have martyrized him on the one and only day that would in the minds of mankind ineffaceably symbolize him as a type of Christ. Understand the story for what it was, a sentimental, Bible-type legend, and the creation of such a parallel is poetically, beautifully justifiable—though, of course, extremely far-fetched even for fiction.

No, sir, Abraham Lincoln is to be added to Moses and Christ as another myth!

Now, in conclusion, let me take care of some more wishful thinking on your part—what you believe to be the actual name of our country. Admittedly, many people still believe as you do, that there was a colorful adventurer named Amerigo Vespucci and that he gave his name to our land; but this is simply another instance of history being written to fit the fiction required. You say the name Amerigo derives from Amelric, the first Gothic king of Seville. Very neat, because if that can be proved then the literal root-meaning of the name of our land is Kingdom of Heaven, Amel-Ric and Himmel-Reich being identical. Or, alternatively, if Amel be taken as the name of the chief god of the Goths, Amel-Ric means God's Country, Either way you would win. i wish I could believe this, because I do love this wonderful land. But sentiment and reason are generally mutually exclusive, and so here.

You see, friend, a great deal of what has survived of our

American history, is in my opinion pure legend, created by very human poet-patriots, whose burning desire was to show our nation in the most favorable light possible. This feigning was always typical of the minstrels of whatever realm. And so for you this land is the golden land where the Kingdom of Heaven—or God's Country!—is to be realized on earth. Such bosh warms my heart but it splits my head. It's beyond reason. Why, if I could be persuaded to believe this fragrant nonsense I would have to admit that in these latter days—as you call them—history is falling into some predetermined, divine plan: "towards which the whole creation moves."

But that, alas, I can never believe.

As ever,
Your Friend,
Frazer Boughton[1]

---

[1] Reprinted here, thanks to Analog

The End Of Evil

A Dialogue between an Interpreter of prophecy
and a Questioner

Questioner: After reading so many prophecies of doom and destruction I find it hard not to look upon evil as inevitable. Must we then accept something like Calvinism, all the good and evil in the world pre-determined for us — before we are even born?

Interpreter: I hope not.

Q: But if prophecy is a scientific fact — when so many predictions have been amazingly fulfilled — how can we honestly say that man is a free agent able to avoid the evils prophesied?

I: Nevertheless, he is.

Q: But if a prophet — such as Nostradamus — time and again demonstrates his extraordinary gift by the fulfillment of his most circumstantial predictions, does not that lead to the fear that his so far unfulfilled prophecies of wars, earthquakes, plagues and other woes must be likewise fulfilled?

I: Not really. No prophecy is valid until history overtakes it. No matter how wonderful his penned visions, no matter how much confidence they give in those yet to come, nothing but the future itself is judge.

Q: You mean, then, predicted woes can be averted?

I: If man is a free being, they can be. The Book itself, which is filled with prophecies, exhorts us to pray without ceasing — to pray for whatsoever things are good, and pure, and lovely; it tells us that "the fervent, effectual prayer of a righteous man availeth much"; it tells us that "with God all things are possible"; it tells us, "Whether there be prophecies, they shall fail"; it tells us we can avoid "the arrow that flieth by night and the pestilence that walketh at noonday." And at very least, prophecies serve as warnings which let us know what to pray against.

Q: What about those that have already come to pass? I am not as sure of divine protection as you seem to think I am. What troubles me is that when a seer's predictions prove valid the simmering ones may also prove valid. And I don't like some of the things I read. The French were terrified recently over a book on Nostradamus.

I: The French are never terrified. But let me suggest a hope to you. Up to a point we do seem to be robots of history. But is it not receivable that Nostradamus, true seer though he was, may have carried his gift only to that point in time where man's history is forewritten so long as man lets himself be a robot, but not from the moment he begins to recognize himself as in the image and likeness of God. Besides, and I admit this is speculation, I have noticed a basic difference between some of the Bible prophecies and those of Nostradamus. In the former there is a great deal of symbolism, which makes for flexibility of interpretation. It makes as though God were saying: "You have choice between good and evil, even as you read these visions. So choose the good and not the ill." Never look upon evil as a future certainty. Take the predictions of ill as forewarnings of *something to be prayed against*. With God all things are possible, and all means all. Once man repudiates his ingrained gnosticism, evil will flee earth and the Kingdom of Heaven will come down to man.

Q: By repudiating gnosticism? Wasn't gnosticism a heresy of the early Church?

I: It was indeed, and it is rampant today.[1] But weed it out of your thinking and you will no longer worry about prophecies of ill.

Q: I've never studied Church history. Just what is gnosticism?

I: A pessimistic concept that evil is real and eternal, and therefore indestructible, and that it can never be wiped out, only sidestepped as it juggernauts. Such a belief won't help you in your fears of events either present or on the way.

Q: No doubt of that. But what you say doesn't sound quite correct. I was listening the other night on the radio to a professional anti-cultist, and he told his listeners that Christian Science is gnostic — yet everybody knows that this religion *denies* the reality of evil outright.

I: Any encyclopaedia at his elbow would have set him straight. The one thing all gnostics had in common was *dualism*. They believed both good and evil to be eternal, and ditto both matter and Spirit. Which is about as far as you can get from Christian Science. Hans Jonas, authority on gnosticism, says: "To the gnostic, matter was real and an attacker." These pessimists accepted prophecies of doom with alacrity. Church historian William Moore, in his edition of Gregory of Nyssa, says: "With them evil was some inevitable result of the Divine processes; it abode at all events in matter, and human responsibility was at an end." Gerald Bonner, biographer of St. Augustine, states they believed "the divine has fallen into the prison of matter," in other words, that there is life and intelligence in matter. According to George Bishop they held "a dualism impossible in Christian Science."

Q: I like them already. They didn't spout any nonsense about the unreality of evil!

I: If evil is real, who made it?

Q: Oh, I know. You want me to say that God made it, on the ground that God made everything. Well, I admit there is "the problem of evil," and I also admit I don't know the answer to it. But *maybe* the fundamentalists are right. They say that though God did not *make* evil He *allows* it so that man can be a free agent and not a robot. God wants man to have an untrammeled moral choice between good and evil.

I: That would make evil essential to man's freedom. I can't accept that. Why not a free choice among various goods? When I was a youngster in Winnipeg a Dr. Louis Erk, who had a wonderful collection of classical phonograph records allowed me to visit him and play any I liked. I was free to choose, and in my opinion none of his records were bad. So I had complete freedom of choice among many good things. Why should bad things have to be thrown in?

Let's see. The fundamentalist says if there were no evil, man would not have the freedom to choose between good and evil. So what? If there were no apples one would not have the freedom to choose between apples and oranges.

A pessimistic assertion of the necessity of evil was the basic concept of gnosticism, and that monstrous concept poisons much of today's fundamentalism. Imagine! God is supposed to require evil so His Offspring can choose between good and evil! Put this false belief to the test: a monster of a man—who has been allowed God's freedom—waylays, rapes and murders a little girl on her way home from school. He had the freedom to do this dirty deed or not to do it.

Q: Correct.

I: But did the little girl have this freedom?

Q: I understand you. No, she did not. And I admit I have no answer to the problem of evil. But I see it promised in prophecy and I see it all around me. And so, evil is real, and the gnostics were undoubtedly right.

I: Then, keep on worrying about dooms to come. If evil is real you should fear it. And if God made it—because He made everything—you should not try to destroy it. You should never try to destroy anything that God has made.

Q: I couldn't, anyway. So just count me among the gnostics.

I: The Church Fathers were sounder. They were the inheritors of primitive Christianity, which is vastly different from the "Christianity" of today. And that soundness of doctrine lasted long. For at least one thousand five hundred years they maintained as Christianly essential *The Unreality Of Evil.*

Q: I don't believe it!

I: Then let me focus the rays of the sun till they burn.

Q: Go ahead. Which reminds me that what you say about the gnostics — though it seems you have the evidence— seems to contradict what I have heard on the air from the professional anti-cultists. To a man they denounce as a cult any religion that denies the reality of evil.

I: The demagogue Huey Long once jeered: "Sure, we'll have fascism; but we'll call it anti-fascism." Our witch- hunters, too, are demagogues, but their topic is different. And unfortunately, though they are extremist examples, they represent too much of so-called Christian thought today. I am reminded how, in one of his later books, L. Frank Baum relates how the Tin Woodman became tin. He was once a flesh-and-blood human being. But he fell in love with a pretty Munchkin girl in the service of a wicked witch. The witch, not wishing to lose her servant, enchanted the woodman's axe, so that once when out chopping, he chopped off an arm. He straightway went to a tinsmith and had his arm replaced with a tin arm. When next out chopping he chopped off his other arm. This he also had replaced. Well, to make a long story short, he wound up all tin.

Q: How would you prove that the Christian Church is now gnostic?

I: Easily. The witch-hunters attack Christian Science in the identical way the gnostic heretics attacked the Fathers' established doctrine of the *Unreality Of Evil.*

For instance, the *Oxford Dictionary of the Christian Church* (Oxford University Press), under Christian Science, gnostically asseverates: "Its teaching on the unreality of matter, sin and suffering conflicts with the Biblical doctrine of Creation, Fall and Redemption." Shame, my university! And fundamentalist Hoekema quotes, in disapproval: "For Christian Science, evil is nothing, unreal, an illusion and a false belief." While J. Oswald Sanders, in his *Cults and Isms,* is shocked when Mrs. Eddy writes: "If God or good is real, then evil, the unlikeness of God, is unreal." Another holier-than-thou critic, J. L. Neve, in his *Churches and Sects of Christianity.* under s section entitled "Departures from Christianity," remarks, "All Christian Science teaching is based on the assertion that no form of evil possesses the nature of substance." To him and to the other fundamentalists evil is unquestionably a substance.

Q: And it wasn't, to the Fathers?

I: Bishop Hippolytus, recognized as "a zealous defender of the Faith," and who died a martyr's death, in combating the gnostics, said: "Evil is not a substance; it is not a thing at all. It is, literally, nothing. Evil is simply a privation of good." And St. Augustine, in his anti-Manichaean writings is equally postitive: "Evil is no substance." "Evil is the disagreement, which is certainly not a substance." "Evil is not a substance, but a disagreement, hostile to substance."

Biographer of St. Augustine, Anne Freemantle, in her *The Age of Belief,* relates that after nine years of gnosticism this illustrious Father joined the mainstream Christian believers, and at this point she summarizes what they believed, in contradistinction from the gnostics: "Evil, for the Christian, not being created by God, does not really exist, *is not,* since all that is, is good." And according to Albert H. Newman, D.D., "St. Augustine never wearied of assailing this citadel of the gnostic system—reality of evil."

Q: Did the gnostics ever strike back?

 I: Yes. Exactly the way the witch-hunters of today strike back. Augustine reports that Manichee or Manes, the gnostic leader, "thought to demonstrate the positive existence of evil by inviting his opponent to take hold of a scorpion: if he did this, he would be convinced not by words but by brute fact that evil is a substance." Exactly what a "common sense" fundamentalist would say.

Q: How did Augustine answer that one?

 I: It had already been answered centuries earlier by St. Paul, who, bitten by a scorpion, shook it off and felt no hurt.

 Q: Which required a lot of faith—if the story is true.

 I: Or the actual knowledge that evil is only an illusion.

Q: Mrs. Eddy would have liked Augustine.

 I: It is on record that she did. Interestingly, one church historian, Dean Willard L. Sperry, notes with amused surprise that a certain entire chapter on the unreality of evil in Augustine's *Confessions* could be fitted into *Science and Health.*

Q: *Now,* is it *possible* that Augustine *was* heretical among the Fathers in this *one* doctrine of the unreality of evil? A curious quirk, for instance?

 I: In this *fundamental* doctrine he was *highly* representative of orthodox Christianity.

Q: Then wherever you look in the writings of the Fathers you will find this doctrine stated?

 I: Yes. Just the other day, almost at random, I picked up a biography of Luther by Richard Marius, and read this: "At least since Augustine Christians had thought that all being was good by nature. Sin was a lack of something rather than anything positive in itself, just as darkness is an absence of light, and sickness is an absence of health." Take Gregory of Nazianzen, who was among the "champions of orthodoxy." I particularly like to quote: "Evil has no positive existence, but is a negation of good... Sin itself is not a thing, and consequently not a creation. God is indeed the Author of all that is, of every substance; but sin is not a substance and is not." Yet here are these Oxford sciolists, in an ostensibly authoritative book on what Christianity should be, informing us it is heresy to believe sin and evil unreal. But, as I said before, they are today's gnostics. The entire Church which stemmed from Jesus Himself, refutes them. Here are some examples to rub into the minds of the leaders of our great Apostasy.

St, Basil, in his Hekaemeron, says: "It is impious to say that evil has its origin from God, because the contrary cannot proceed from its contrary. Life does not engender death;darkness is not the origin of light; sickness is not the maker of health."

The beloved St. Anselm was and is recognized as of sound doctrine. He was the founder of scholasticism and "the greatest representative of medieval Augustinism." In a chapter headed *Evil, Which Sin Or Injustice Is, Is Nothing,* he writes: "We understand that evil is nothing. For just as injustice is nothing but the absence of due justice, so evil is nothing but the absence of due good...Evil, in so far as it is injustice, is always nothing, beyond any doubt. ...At times it seems to be something, as in the case of pain and grief." It only *seems.*

Q: Amazing! The Oxford University gnostics should have hunted him down for his denial of the reality of sin!

I: They should have read up on Church history. But apparently Anselm is in Paradiso now, among the spirits of light and power "in the sphere of the Sun." Dante put him there, an eternal honor! And Pope Clement XI canonized him, so his orthodoxy was affirmed, despite our gnostic anti-cultists.

Q: So, I see the Fathers denied the reality of sin, as well as of evil!

I: Of course. Because sin is an aspect of evil. The root of the word itself points to its native nothingness. Sin, literally, means *missing the mark.* St. Gregory of Nyssa, orthodox of orthodox, in a letter to Eustathia, explains: "Sin, indeed, is a miscarriage, not a quality of, human nature; just as disease and deformity are not congenital to it in the first instance, but are its unnatural accretions, activity in the direction of sin is to be thought of as a mere mutilation of the goodness innate in us; *It Is Not Found To Be Itself A Real Thing*, but we see it only in the absence of that goodness."

So you see, then, it is the fundamentalists who are the gnostic heretics, in opposition to the mainstream Church Fathers.

Q: Let me catch my breath! You are telling me that the fundamentalists, in granting Satan power, are placing themselves in the position of the gnostic heretics who affirmed the reality of evil — including sin — in opposition to the Fathers who asserted doctrinally and dogmatically that only good is real. You have something here fit for Ripley's *Believe it or Not*. I am sure the fundamentalists are not in the least aware of the authenticity of this mainstream Church doctrine or they would not attack it as heresy.

I: They are apparently totally ignorant of it. But this doctrine is a necessary corollary of the affirmation of the Omnipotence and Omnipresence of God.

Q: What about the Church Councils? Did they ever give the *Unreality Of Evil* doctrine their seal of approval?

I: Indeed they did. At the Synod of Braga in Portugal, 561 A.D. they asserted: "Everything that is, is good because it comes from the one Creator." And at the Council of Florence (1439-1442 A.D.) nearly a thousand years later they were still declaring: "The Church asserts that there is no such thing as a nature of evil, because every nature, insofar as it is a nature, is good." The Fathers were sun-clear on their position. "Evil," said St. John of Damascus, "is nothing else than absence of goodness, just as darkness also is absence of light."

Q: Very well. Now I understand what you meant when you said, "Don't be a gnostic."

I: Fine! It doesn't matter whether the evil you fear is present, nearby or in unfulfilled but simmering prophecy. Deny it. Gregory of Nazianzen, thoroughly orthodox, put it well: "Good is the only reality; evil is the negative, the non-existent, and must finally abolish itself, because it is not of God." The Trinitarian Boethius writes: "Can God do evil? No. Wherefore, evil is nothing, since He cannot do it who can do anything." St. Athanasius, of the Athanasian Creed, in *Con-*

tra Gentes, writes: "But good is, while evil is not . . . By what is not I mean what is evil, insofar as it consists in a false imagination in the thoughts of men . . . It is a false view that evil is something in the nature of things, and has substantive existence." Dionysius the Areopagite, a favorite of the Fathers, says: "Evil does not reside in matter; in fact it has no real existence anywhere and no efficient cause . . . Nothing is real unless it partakes of good. Insofar as good is lacking, reality is lacking." And according to St. Thomas Aquinas: "The fundamental truth is expressed by Dionysius: 'Evil has no existence . . . If the perfection and the being of all things are goods, it follows that the opposite to good, i.e. evil, has neither perfection nor being . . . Evil is, therefore, if we may so express it, a purely negative reality; more correctly, it has no degree of either essence or reality."

Q: Why, then, do the professional anti-cultists attack a religion that holds the same anti-evil doctrine as do the Fathers?

I: Because they are theological illiterates.

Q: But they must read *some* books!

I: Not those that puncture their bubbles. Can you imagine them, during one of their attacks, daring to quote Bishop Hippolytus, who orthodoxly affirms, "All good is from God. All things are good, and that which is nothing cannot be known." Or the Summa: "Every being, as being, is good. In the degree that it exists, it is good." This mighty, all-important truth is a never-ending refrain in the Fathers. But the anti- cultists, though they bow in mighty respect to these mainstream Christians, have forborne to turn their pages.

Q: But if evil is unreal, as the Fathers insist, what about the reality of his coming Royal Highness, the uppity antichrist? If he arrives to trample his way through the nations can we overcome him merely by unseeing him, by saying there's no such thing as evil?

I: By just *saying* it? Not at all. But by *knowing* it? Yes. But as long as we accept the reality of evil, we will find plenty of evil to accept. In the degree we believe in evil, to that same degree we cancel belief in God as omnipresent and omnipotent. I prefer Clement of Alexandria: "Nothing withstands God: nothing opposes Him; seeing that He is Lord and omnipotent." Or that magnificent monograph, The

Shepherd of Hermas, read regularly for centuries in the primitive Church: "Fearing the Lord, you will have dominion over the devil, for there is no power in Him." And Augustine, too, put it beautifully, in his *City of God*: "There is no entity contrary to the divine, because nonentity seems to be that which is wholly opposite to Him who supremely and always is . . . To that nature which supremely is, and which created all else that exists, no nature is contrary save that which does not exist. For nonentity is the contrary of that which is. And thus there is no being contrary to God, the Supreme Being, Author of all beings whatsoever . . . To God no evils are hurtful."

Q: So "the true serpent," as you say Nostradamus calls the coming antichrist, cannot hurt us?

I: Exactly. Because, as Augustine says: "All things are good."

Recently I was reading Church Father Cassian's Conferences, and I think he has something for you. In Chapter Six of his book, under the heading of *The Fact That Nothing Is Created Evil By God*, he writes relevantly to our discussion:

> God forbid that we should admit that God has created anything which is substantially evil, as the Scripture says, 'Everything that God had made was very good.' For if they were created by God such as they are now, or made for this purpose; namely, to occupy these positions of malice, and ever to be ready for the deception and ruin of men, we should, in opposition to the view of the above quoted by Scripture, slander God as the Creator and author of evil, as having Himself formed utterly evil wills and natures, creating them for this very purpose; namely, that they might ever persist in wickedness and never pass over to a feeling of good will.

Q: Wouldn't you hate the anti-Christ as evil if he arrives?

I: It might be difficult not to; but I would prefer to think like St. Clement, who said, "There is nothing in existence for which God is not the Cause. It must be, then, that there is nothing that God hates, nothing that the Word Hates."

Q: I'm beginning to think that there is a certain namby-pamby goody-goody element among your saintly Fathers.

I: Goody-goody, if you like. But not namby-pamby. They met martyrdom with incredible heroism, because they knew what

Truth is. They saw Reality. They saw it through the cloud.

Q: Now I understand what you mean when you say, "Don't be a gnostic." But I simply would never be able to take a steady look at a Hitler-type and affirm that "he's God's child."

I: Even the reverend Walter Martin has been able to do that.

Q: What do you mean? He's an anti-cultist and denounces that type of thinking.

I: Yes, I know. The type of thinking of St. Augustine and St. Athanasius. But he yielded to it at least once—I have it on tape. He admitted that man is basically good, when he said to a caller-in, "The *real* you is perfect." A sublime truth! Knowing that truth can heal the sick, whether mentally or physically. When Jesus looked at a cripple or a blind man, or a deaf man he knew that "the real you is the image and likeness of God." And that knowledge straightway healed the sick. And it raised the dead.

"Man was not intended to die," said St. Athanasius.

Q: But man will not overcome death by denying its reality, will he?

I: Indeed he will.

Q: Jesus never denied the reality of death.

I: Oh yes he did. On at least two occasions. And he was laughed at for this denial of error. Dr. S. I. McMillan writes: "When Jesus told those who were mourning over the dead body of Jairus' daughter, 'she is not dead, but sleepeth,' they ridiculed Him with scornful epithets." But he refuted their materialism by raising her up. Said Athanasius, "Life does not die, but quickens the dead."

Likewise with Lazarus. When he was known to be dead Jesus said of him, "Our friend Lazarus sleepeth; but I go, that I may awake him out of sleep." The disciples thought that he did not understand the situation, apparently. But then "said Jesus to them plainly, Lazarus is dead." Comments golden-tongued St. Chrysostom: "Observe how he leadeth Mary's mind upward; for to raise Lazarus was not the only thing sought; it was necessary that both she and they who were with her should learn the Resurrection. Wherefore, before the raising of the dead he teacheth heavenly wisdom by words. But if he is the Resurrection and the Life, He is not confined by place, but, present everywhere, knoweth how to heal . . . What he saith is of this kind: 'Neither is this man dead, nor shall he die.'" And Athanasius, commenting on this same resurrection, elucidates: "It came to pass that Lazarus fell sick and died; but the divine Man did not fall sick . . ."

Q: O. K. The antichrist, too, will be sick. Can we heal him?

I: Yes, even he is healable. Look again for the "real you." We should see him as a child of good, not evil by nature. The Fathers agreed with Aristotle: "The true nature of anything is the best that it can grow into." Augustine agreed: "For no nature at all is evil, and this is a name for nothing but the want of good . . . Not even the nature of the devil himself is evil, insofar as it is nature." Let the human race know this and "the true serpent" will vanish like a puff of smoke. Said Boethius: "The power of doing evil is no power at all . . . All that falls away from the good, ceases also to exist." It matters not whether the evil you fear is an evil predicted or an evil present. Deny it. It is illusion only.

Q: So everything is *maya!* As in Hinduism!

I: Not at all. Only evil. Why think good *maya*, since God made good and not evil? The very name God means good. But "we see through a glass darkly," said Paul. And according to St. Athanasius mortal "man is made out of what is not." Melito calls mortal existence "error." St. John of Avila calls it "a delusion." Aquinas calls it "phantasmal." Augustine quotes the Areopagite with approval: "All human thought is a kind of error, when tried by the stability and durability of the Divine and most perfect conceptions." Cassian calls it "our illusion." St. Ignatius calls it "the error of evil." Even our own thunderer Jonathan Edwards affirms: "The Material Universe exists only in the mind."

Q: You certainly have rounded up an imposing list of mainstream religionists who deny matter's reality and who label it illusion. I am truly surprised, because I thought it was only the Christian Scientists who did so.

I: No. It was the entire mainstream Church who denied the reality of matter and evil and it was their deadly foes the gnostics who insisted that matter and evil are substance.

Q: But how did the gnostics explain this evil?

I: They had ready answers. Either there was a split in the Godhead itself (the most accepted gnostic view) or (for those among them who did not like the idea of a good God creating evil) there were two Gods, the good one creating good and the evil one creating evil. Simple!

Q: I still like the common sense of the gnostics. For how can we honestly deny the evil we see all around us? And I don't see how that Christian Science type of thinking can help us if an antichrist arrives. The other day I was reading a new book by Dave Hunt and he was saying that when antichrist hits the scene the Christian Scientists, with their Pollyanna type of thinking and blinders before their eyes will go along with him in all his atrocities. In fact, I have the book here. Let me quote the passage:

> To those in 'higher' states of consciousness under Antichrist's hypnotic control, the slaughter of millions will not have happened. Christian Scientists . . . will se no evil at all during the entire Great Tribulation, for Antichrist will help them to see only good.

Strong words! Then, did the Christian Scientists collaborate with Hitler, seeing no evil in *him?* It sounds as though they would have!

I: On the contrary. Hitler closed all the Christian Science churches in Germany, confiscated all the church property and sent Christian Scientists to concentration camps for being Christian Scientists. The Nazi doctors accused them of faith healing and occultism, so said Heydrich, and added that their denial of material existence put them into opposition to the National Socialist Weltanschauung. They were also accused of being anti-racist and quoted Mrs. Eddy's statement: "No inherent qualities of race exist."

The entire family of Count Moltke became Christian Scientists, to such a degree that it was amusedly stated that even their horses were healed by prayer. One of Moltke's Christian Science sons was a part of the putsch against Hitler and was executed. The fundamentalists did much better under Hitler. To them it was "Why worry about persecution of the Jews: they are going to hell anyway." And, let me add, if you want to know whether a fundamentalist has God or Satan for his Deity, ask him simply: "Where are the six million Jews?"

Q: Nevertheless,if another Hitler ever arrives can we call him a phantom? Can we make him unreal by taking thought?

I: No. We won't be *making* him unreal, we will be *recognizing* his unreality. Otherwise he will be unconquerable. The trouble could be a possible mass acceptance of his power to do evil. But Augustine is right: "The power to do evil is no power at all." *Nationwide Or Worldwide Prayer Could Take Care Of Him.*

Q: By recognizing his non-existence?

I: By recognizing the non-existence of anything whatsoever not made by the God who made all things and who made them good. Are these words not golden?: "Whatsoever things you ask for when you pray, believe that you *have* received them and you *shall* have them." See peace instead of war. See Christ instead of anti-Christ. See eternal good instead of temporal evil. See what you already have, that is, open your genuine eyes to the visible presence of the Kingdom of Heaven. It is right here.

Q: I don't see it around me.

I: Nevertheless it is all around you and me and everybody at this moment. And its reality is soon to be made manifest in this wonderful land of ours, this Manasseh!

Q: Why *this* land?

I: *First* of all.

Q: And why first?

I: Did you know that the very name, "America", means "Kingdom of Heaven"? Literally.

Q: Literally? How so?

I: The name America comes from the first name of Amerigo Vespucci, the cartographer.

Q: So?

I: And his name of Amerigo came from his Gothic ancestors, who were named Amelric. And *Amelric* in Gothic is identical to Kingdom of Heaven. Here is no chance coincidence, but destiny.

Q: Does Nostradamus say anything about this coming kingdom?

I: I believe he does. He prophesies:

Libra will see the lands of the West reign,
Holding the monarchy of heaven and earth:
No one will see the forces of Asia perish,
So that seven will not hold the hierarchy in order.

(IV, 50)

Libra verra regner les Hesperies,
De ciel et terre tenir la monarchie:
D'Asie forces nul ne verra péries,
Que sept ne tiennent par rang la hiérarchi:.

We are the Westerners, so two lines are clear. What the
rest mean, I do not know. It has been suggested that a destruction so utter will overtake Asia that there will be no
one left alive to describe it. I hope not. The last line needs
a nearer time to be understood.

Q: Does Nostradamus predict anything more for us?

I: Yes. And apparently he was the first man in the history of
the world to pen the words "Government of America." Nostradamus lived from 1503 to 1566 and there was no government of America when he wrote. Even the first colonists
hadn't arrived here.

Q: What did he prophesy?

I:
There will be a head of London from the government of America
Isle of Scotland, he will pave you with ice;
They will have Reb for king, a very false anti-Christ,
Who will put them all in an uproar.

(10.66)

Le chef de Londres par regne l'Americh,
L'Isle d'Ecosse t'empiera par gelée;
Roy Reb auront, un si faux Antechrist,
Qui les mettra trestous dans la meslée.

To me, the quatrain suggests an Anglo-Saxon federation
of England and America. According to the Anglo-Israel interpretation of Bible prophecy such a federation will certainly take place, Israel being literally and mainly the
British Isles and our land. A vast theme—and for a later
book. Who Reb is we cannot know till the appointed time.
"A very false anti-Christ" is a puzzler. What is a false Christ?
An anti-Christ? Possibly, one falsely called anti-Christ is

meant here, because a false Christ and false anti-Christ should not mean the same thing, and Nostradamus is not a word-waster. The number of the quatrain, 1066, may be a subtlety indicating that in this great federation the Isles are to play a part subordinate to America. Nostradamus also predicts elsewhere that the headquarters of the British government will be in our land.

Q: Is this supposed to take place before or after the arrival of the Arab anti-Christ, as you call him.

I: I do not know yet, but I believe they will both arrive in the same generation.

Q: Very well then. Now, to get back to the positive thinking and Church Father doctrine that evil does not really exist. Suppose the Arab or otherwise anti-Christ has actually arrived. What are we going to do about him? Let's say that the evil he manifests is illusion and that we pray by trying to see him as a child of God? That didn't work with Hitler.

I: We didn't try it with Hitler.

Q: I don't see how what to me is a Pollyanna affirmation can destroy such a manifestation of evil. I would prefer to "praise the Lord and pass the ammunition."

I: Ammunition may not work. As I see it, from collating Bible and extra-Bible prophecies bullets may not be able to harm him. He is described as a wonder-worker—"of the league of the great Hermes"—and my speculation is (and I emphasize the word *speculation*) he will wield an extraordinary control of matter based on his knowledge that matter is, quite literally, an object of thought only and not a substance. To have achieved this power he may be very ascetic or "spiritual" — I use the term spiritual here as the Bible uses it once when referring to "spiritual wickedness in high places." His control of matter will then not stem from any positive spirituality but from an overwhelming and all-consuming ego-push. The concept of anti-Christ or Lucifer avers an ego apart from God, and there is and can be no ego apart from God. But average man, not accustomed to miracles, may think him a God- like being because he produces wonders which, though actual, are self-aggrandizing.

Q: Will he do what Jesus did, heal the sick and raise the dead?

I: I do not know. But nothing in the Bible prophecies indicate that he will. He is described as working wonders—and as able to call down fire from heaven. Though, oddly, the coming "Elijah" should also be able to do this.

Q: Hitler did that with his bombers.

I: That was not unique. We did it too, and to even more deadly effect. We were as anti-Christ as anyone could be when we wiped out two Japanese cities, including all men, women and children; and at a time when both we and our foe knew they had lost the war and would have given up soon thereafter. No, there will be something unique about the "true serpent," as Nostradamus calls him. But he can and will be destroyed when we spiritually understand two powerful doctrines of the true Church.

Q: What are they?

I: The Fathers also denied the reality of matter. They knew—even more clearly than will the anti-Christ—that there is no substance or reality in matter and that it is basically illusion.

Q: Then the Oxford scholars who disapproved of disbelief in matter should go after the Fathers as heretical here too!

I: Yes, those gnostics should. And to be consistent they should witch-hunt after Bishop Berkeley, Jonathan Edwards, and C. S. Lewis!

Q: C. S. Lewis! Did he believe matter unreal?

I: Yes. He was completely convinced by Berkeley's reasoning.

Q: And the church fathers? That's hard to believe!"

I: Yet it is undeniably so. In their manifold writings against the gnostics they accused them of believing in life, truth and intelligence in matter. Orthodox Bishop Alexander of Lycopolis, for instance, exclaimed against them: "They say that God sent virtue into matter. But the things which are with God admit of no fellowship with matter . . . They hold that evil is a material substance, equal and opposite to good." And Tertullian, formulator of the Trinity, in his anti-gnostic manifesto scoffed: "They will have it that God made all things out of matter . . . They give divine attributes to matter and so make two Gods! *But Matter Is Nowhere!*" And St. Gregory of Nazianzen, defender of the Faith, warned: "Flee from the matter and darkness of Manes!" And martyr Bishop Methodius jeered at the gnostics, "You wish for the existence of matter!" And the great St. Thomas of Aquinas, in a chapter heading of his Summa, affirms: *In God There Is No Matter.*

Q: But if matter doesn't exist, what did they think God made the world of?

I: From the beginning, and for centuries, orthodox Church doctrine affirmed that God made the world out of nothing.

Q: So He took some nothing and made the world and man?

I: No. Bishop Hippolytus said: "The gnostics lay down two principles, God and matter. And yet God does not stand in need of matter to make things, since in His Mind all things substantially exist." Or, as St. John of Damascus, in his Exposition of the Orthodox Faith affirmed,"It is by thought that He creates, and thought is the basis of His work."

Q: Are you pulling my leg? It sounds exactly like a New Age doctrine.

I: That's not my problem; but it will be a problem of today's fundamentalists. Let us ask them why they have gone gnostic.

Q: You quote an impressive number of orthodox Church Fathers; and they do seem to be voicing what they believed to be sound doctrine. But you have not quoted St. Augustine, who I do believe, was considered, possibly, the greatest and most authoritative of the Fathers in matters doctrinal. Was he in line with them?

I: In perfect line. In his earlier years he had been a gnostic - for nine years, actually! And after he became an orthodox Christian he stated of the heretics: "They could conceive of no non-material existence."

Q: So he condemned their belief in the reality of matter?

I: Unmistabably. He asserted, "Matter in itself can neither have being nor be known."

Q:You know, one thing amazes me about all this. The evidence seems to be clear that the mainstream Christian Church doctrinally denied the reality of evil and of matter. Yet much of the so-called Christian Church today condemns any religion that holds those same two doctrines.

I: I told you why: because the Christian Church has gone gnostic. And to the degree it has done so it will be fit fodder for the predicted anti-Christ and his cohorts. Or for any anti-Christ at any time. Because it cannot believe that the anti-Christ has any power whatsoever and *at the same time* maintain that God has all-power! The Church has forfeited God's omnipotent help when it deems omni-potence but a word. The great Apostasy is here.

Q: If this prophesied wonder-worker comes do you think he will hold to the unreality of matter and manipulate the illusion by the power of his mind?

I: This seems to be indicated in prophecy, as I have already said. If so, he may have the edge over us for a while. If we take his illusions for reality we cannot properly fight them or him. So, again, I repeat, and again and again, *Don't be a gnostic*. That way lies destruction. Learn the *reality* of good and the unreality of anything that vaunts itself against the infinitely good and everywhere present Father of all. In his treatise on Faith and the Creed Augustine had some wise words applicable to the false Christ: He said that just as cold is contrary to hot, and quick is contrary to slow, that *which is not* is contrary to That Which Is. "There cannot possibly exist any nature contrary to God," he affirmed. We, too, should use that thought as an affirmation, if "the true serpent"comes.

Q: Do you really believe that just by looking at him and his evil antics and seeing him as a child of God and affirming the unreality of evil that this will wipe him off the world scene?

I: I believe so. Especially if we pray en masse. But if the witless hullabaloo over a simple and harmless prayer in school is any index this may not be too easily achieved. John Gimenez, a religionist I heard recently on television, put it well: "If we ever prayed together at one time the heavens would shake." They would. And they would shake out anti-Christ into the bottomless pit of his native nothingness. Then would follow the prophesied restoration of all things.

Q; Did Nostradamus include that among his predictions?

I: he did indeed. He has penned two quatrains on what seems to me to be *The Ultimate:*

The body without soul no longer to be as a sacrifice,
Day of death to become day of birth:
The divine spirit will make the soul happy,
Seeing the Word in its eternity.

(2.13)

Jesus, who overcame death for others and for himself prophesied that someday those who followed his teachings would do greater works than he. Greater? What could be greater? But at any rate there would have to be more conquests of death — at the least; and according to Nostradamus, this will literally occur. He says:

At the revolution of the great number seven.
It will happen, in the time of the games of the hecatomb,
Not far from the great age thousand
That the dead will arise from their tombs.

(10.74)

Au revolu du grand nombre septieme
Apparoistra, autemps jeux d'Hecatombe:
Non esloigne du grand aage miliesme,
Que les entrez sortiront de leur tombe.

In my first book on Nostradamus, published by Scribner, I commented:

According to the Biblical calculations of our seer the world was almost five thousand years old with the advent of Jesus Christ. Two thousand years added to that figure gives "the revolution of the great number seven "near" the great age thousand," i.e., the seventh revolution of the year thousand since creation.

"Games of the hecatomb" is still a mystery: we are apparently not near enough to the assigned time for the fulfillment of this prophecy, which is to be around the year 2000 A.D.

The last line is a prediction of an extraordinary event or series of events: "The dead will arise from their tombs." We may recall Jeses' prophecy that the time would come when Christians would perform greater works than the master himself. Among other things, these works will include not only healing the sick but raising the dead.

Man, born again — that is, spiritually, with a spiritual body — and completely blessed will see the Word or God expressed as son in His full glory.

The other prophecy reads:

The divine word will give to substance
comprising heaven, earth, hidden gold, mystical fact
Body, soul, spirit having all power,
As much under its feet as in the heavenly seat.

(3.2)

The Divine Logos, i.e., God as Creator and expression, pours forth on all things the riches of His All-comprising substance. Thereby, man, now become the embodiment or expression of Spirit, Soul, God is blessed with dominion over all things.

This state of infinite perfection and power is not attained by dying and "going to heaven," because "there is as much under its feet as in the heavenly seat." "As in heaven , so on earth. " Man does not go to heaven: heaven is brought down to earth. Man, total man, comprising body, soul, spirit, will literally have "all power." He will be able to say to yonder mountain, "Be thou removed and cast into the sea."

Q: Literally?

I: Literally. He will know that the mountain is only an object of thought and subject to the one aware of that powerful fact. And it will be equally easy for him to defuse an atom bomb intended for his destruction. On the other hand he may be able to explode in our faces an atom bomb of our own. I mean antichrist.

Q: Then how on earth will we be able to destroy him?

I: Ask rather how in heaven will we be able to do this. As I said before, by the united power of prayer. Take, for instance, Trinity Broadcasting, which already accepts the healing Christ. Suppose that millions tuning in on that wide network were informed that now is the time to pray for a specific good for the world, don't you think that powerhouse could unleash a Christ power that would help heal the world? At least, I believe so.

Q: Well, we could try it; and maybe some day we will. We may need to if this man arrives to bring a day of dread. I observe that he could be *not* a good man yet at the same time be able to recognize matter as an illusion. I thought only an ascetic saint could properly do that.

I: The saint overcomes matter and works his "miracles" by being a channel for the power of God. But he knows that it is not his human mind that works the beneficent wonders, but the divine Mind. The antichrist, on the other hand, will overcome matter and do his stunts purely for the sake of ego. He need not be a saint to be ascetic. One can be an ascetic villain.

Q: But must this possibly ascetic villain come? Must we go through another holocaust even worse than any we have had?

I: In my opinion, *not necessarily.*

Q: Then what about all the prophecies you interpret, both Nostradamus and the Bible? Especially the latter. If the prophecies are in the Bible, don't they have to be fulfilled?

I: No, because the Bible also teaches that man's will is free. But if all its prophecies are inevitable how can man be other than a robot or an actor on moving celluloid? The answer is in the Bible itself. Paul says: "Whether there be prophecies, they shall fail...But love never faileth.".

You have that book of Dave Hunt in your hand. there is much in it that I totally disagree with. But though a fundamentalist he is also that rare bird, a man of hope, and at the close of his book he has a paragraph that is simply magnificent. Let me have it. Here we are:

> Although it may seem unlikely to succeed, we are to attempt to persuade the entire human race to renounce the Lie and embrace the truth. Yes , the prophecies pronouncing judgment on this earth are unequivocal. But so was the judgment that God told Jonah to denounce against Nineveh: 'Yet forty days and Nineveh will be overthrown!' Nothing could be more clearly stated than that —yet Nineveh was not destroyed in forty days or even forty years. Why? God has promised, "If that nation against which I have spoken turns from its evil, I will relent concerning the calamity I planned to bring on it." Nineveh repented and was spared. We must work, persuade, pray to God, and plead with unbelievers everywhere to repent and ask God to spare this world its holocaust. On the other hand, if so many people refuse to repent that the holocaust comes as prophesied, at least we have rescued millions who, because of their repentance and faith in Jesus Christ, will not be part of it. That is something well worth expending our lives for.[2]

Solid, sincere and *true* words. Individual and mass prayer, individual repentance, knowing that God is all good and right here will succeed in bringing the Kingdom of Heaven to earth. Let us repeat Paul's words: "Whether there be prophecies, they shall fail. But love never faileth." "All things are possible to him that believeth." And the good we ask for is *already* ours. We must know that we *have* received that for which we pray. The kingdom of heaven is among us right now and we need but to open our eyes to that present and sublime reality. The world will then appear in its truth, in the image and likeness of the One altogether lovely. Prayer without ceasing is a serene attitude that understands that there is only one power and plan in the universe.

Prayer is Excalibur.

---

[1] Jean Guitton, Professor of the Sorbonne, church historian, in *Great Heresies and Church Councils,* states: "Gnosticism attacked the very essence of the message: the idea of the Good News proclaimed to all.

"Gnosticism also corrupted the essence of doctrine. It attacked the religion of love at the point where it is forever vulnerable: the existence of evil. Had Jesus conquered evil? Can we believe in Jesus, Son of God, and yet accept within and all around us the shattering and undeniable fact of evil?

"Now that the end of the 20th century is drawing closer, these few words will suffice to convince the reader that gnosticism still has currency, to make us realize that it lives on, concealed or else unconsciously, in not a few minds of the present."

And Mrs. Eddy has warned: "Unless a great and radical change is effected by pure Christianity our Cause will disappear and the schools of Gnosticism and Theosophy will take the place of Christian Science,"

[2] From the book entitled, *Peace, Prosperity And The Coming Holocaust.*

When Is The Second Coming?

Religionists who believe that Jesus is coming soon — and some of whom dance up and down with joy at the thought — are altogether too sanguine. Jesus is coming, but He is not coming soon. Certain Scriptural Prophecies must first be fulfilled, and they cover quite a spread of time.

Those who believe that Jesus will soon be here are blindly ignoring plainly-writ Holy Writ. One prophecy reads:

> Elijah shall first come and restore all things.

The herald of the First Advent was John the Baptist, whom Jesus dubbed "Elijah."

And there is to be an "Elijah", herald of the *Second* Advent, and he has not yet arrived. He is promised in the last two verses of the last book of the Old Testament:

> Behold, I will send you Elijah the prophet before the coming of the great and terrible day of the Lord:
> And *He* shall turn the heart of the fathers to the children, and the heart of the children to their fathers, lest I come and smite the earth with a curse.

John has said of him whom Elijah precedes:

> When *He* shall appear we shall be like him, for we shall see him as he is.

Are we like *Him*? Look around the world. Look at Central America. Look at Europe. Look at the Middle East. Look at ourselves. Like Him? No. We are not rapture-ready.

And included in the prophesied pre-Advent period is the restoration of the twelve tribes of Israel under David. The prophet Hosea previews the latter days of our century.

Yet the number of the children of Israel shall be as the sand of the sea, which cannot be measured nor numbered; and it shall come to pass, that in the place where it was said unto them, ye are not my people, there it shall be said unto them, ye are the sons of the living God.

Then shall the children of Judah and the children of Israel be gathered together, and appoint themselves one head, and they shall come up out of the land:
For great shall be the day of Jezreel.

And God, speaking through Ezekiel, tells us of this same restoration preceding the Second Coming:

And I will set up one shepherd over them, and he shall feed them, even my servant David; he shall feed them. And he shall be their servant.
And I the Lord will be their God, and my servant David a prince among them; I the Lord have spoken it.
And I will make with them a covenant of peace, and will cause the evil beasts to cease out of the land: and they shall dwell safely in the wilderness, and sleep in the woods.
And I will make them and the places round about my hill a blessing; and I will cause the shower to come down in his season; there shall be showers of blessing.
And the tree of the field shall yield her fruit, and the earth shall yield her increase, and they shall be safe in their land, and shall know that I am the Lord.
When I have broken the bands of their yoke, and delivered them out of the hand of those that served themselves of them.
And they shall no more be a prey to the heathen, neither shall the beast of the land devour them; but they shall dwell safely, and none shall make them afraid.

And When Is This Great Restoration?

From ancient Persia (now Iran) comes one vision of the time of the end.

In the latter days, just prior to the destruction of all evil. Soshyos and six of his companions will divide the work among them, and each of them will miraculously communicate with the other of his six colleagues in the other zones. They will read each other's thoughts from a distance and will thus converse just as two men sitting close together would do. The work of the renovation of the world will last for fifty-seven years. All evil will perish during these fifty-seven years[1]

With some interpreters of Bible prophecy these wonderful events already constitute the Second Coming.

To the Church Fathers, Jesus would triumph when he arrived in the hearts of mankind. This view is summarized by Aloys:

> After his earthly life and passion there follows a still more far-reaching transformation. Christ's Second Coming does not therefore take place in human form. His *manhood* seems to be done away with...
>
> Christ can no longer properly be called "man" as the Godhead lays claim to all that is in him. According to Paul in 1 Cor. 5, 16, we may "no longer know Christ after the flesh." for the nature of the flesh has been completely taken up into the spiritual substance (i.e. the Godhead). What was once of man has now been made completely of God. Christ's humanity, then, is not simply dissolved in the Godhead. It has reality, but no longer its earthly *idiomata*... The human element in Christ is no longer shown in natural properties. All is filled with the glory of the Godhead.

Or, as church historian Seeberg states:

> It is one of the most certain facts of history, that the thought and feeling of the apostolic age was based, not upon the man Jesus, but upon the Lord in heaven, who pervades and governs the universe, omnipotent and omniscient.

Certainly it is more of a triumphant Second Coming if Christ takes his prophesied place in the heart and soul of mankind, which is what our Lord lived and suffered for, than that we should expect Jesus to do everything for us, like a flying saucer savior.

Regarding the true Second Coming, St. Augustine was unmistakably clear:

> When He shall appear, we shall be like Him; for we shall see Him as He is." We cannot deny that the sons of God shall see God; but they shall see Him as invisible things are seen...In what other manner are invisible things seen than by the eyes

of the mind?

Perhaps I am a little old-fashioned; for it may be that if the lens of our senses were cleansed so that we no longer see through a glass darkly, we might actually and literally see the real Jesus Christ and not a simulacrum projected by human thought. If so he would then have truly appeared to us. Does not the once- visible literal Lord of earth and heaven still (and always) represent the Father who is infinitely greater than he? And would he not be around when his teachings triumph?

Revelation prophecy has God saying: "Behold, I make all things new." And Scripture counters any thought of evil being eternal. For, if the punishment of the wicked persists eternally, than evil, the reason for the punishment, likewise persists e- ternally.

Ultimately, no trace of a trace of evil will exist anywhere in God's universe (nor does it now, except as illusion). According to prophecy, hell itself is to be annihilated, and it will not exist even as an appearance.

Why?

Because hell is scheduled to suffer the same identical fate as death, of whom it is prophesied:

"The last enemy that shall be destroyed is death." (Jesus)

"There shall be no more death." (St. John)

Will there be even a whiff left of death? No!

Now, perpend: St. John prophetically lumps hell with his pal death for utter destruction:

And death and hell were cast into the lake of fire.

This *lake of fire* is not itself hell or death, but it is to burn up hell and death. Both.

Therefore a blessed time is coming when there will exist neither death nor hell. God shall be All-in-all.

But God already is All-in-all.

Perhaps his Coming, then, is simply the opening of our eyes to his ever-presence.

And when this ever-presence is realized most utterable will be a mundane prayer of Adoration from the Canonical Prayer Book of a faith which claims John the Baptist ("Elijah") as its founder:

Thy name, life, is excellent: its glory is great. Its light abundant. Its goodness overflowed, inaugurating the first mystery, life which proceeded from life and truth which existed before the beginning. This is a wellspring of life which sprang forth from the place of life: we drink thereof, of this fount of life which life transmitted was established in the house of life, which crossed worlds, came, cleft the heavens and was revealed.

Thou hast shown us that which the eye of man hath not seen, and caused us to hear that which human ear has not heard. Thou hast freed us from death and united us with life, released us from darkness and united us with light, led us out of evil and joined us to good. Thou hast shown us the way of life and hast guided our feet into ways of truth and faith so that life cometh and expelleth darkness and goodness cometh and casteth out evil. Like the mingling of wine with water, so may thy truth, thy righteousness and thy faith be added to those who love thy way of truth.

A fitting close for a book on the End of Evils Begun is a wonderful prophecy from the ancient British Druids. When Christianity was first brought to Britain the Druids quickly converted. The Druid priesthood was already monotheistic, and it was patriarchal. A Druid priest was British—, which is Hebrew for Covenant man. He was an early Hebrew arrival to the Isles of the West. For centuries one of his names for God was Yesu. And now his God had arrived.

His thinking was beautiful and totally true:

There is no transgression which will not be set right, no displeasure which will not be forgiven, and no anger which will not be pacified. There is nothing ugly which will not be made beautiful, there is no evil which shall not be removed; there is no desire which shall not be attained. There can be nothing which shall not be known; there can be no loss of anything beloved which shall not be regained;[2] and there can be no end to the blessedness which shall be attained. There is no understanding power and love other than this.

Coming to this entire universe is a glory beyond human conception.

---

[1] St. Bearcan gives hugh the Red sixty years of rule.

[2] Whoever you are, reader: if you have lost a loved one, I know for a fact that

you will see that loved one again. As a psychic researcher of 44 years standing, I say, the evidence for life after death is overwhelming. Have no doubts.

Appendix I

Gnoshing On The Gnostics

In written and cassette attacks on Christian Science Reverend Walter Martin singles out for special disapproval a short, affirmative prayer read in all Christian Science churches and called "The Scientific Statement of Being." It goes thus:

> There is no life, truth, intelligence, nor substance in matter. All is infinite Mind and its infinite manifestation, for God is All-in-all. Spirit is immortal Truth; matter is mortal error. Spirit is the real and eternal; matter is the unreal and temporal. Spirit is God, and man is His image and likeness. Therefore man is not material; he is spiritual.

Concerning the above, Reverend Martin asserts: "With one sweep of the pen Gnosticism came to life again, in the nineteenth century; and Christian Science was born."

Patently untrue.

If "The Scientific Statement of Being" is Gnostic it will match what the early Church Fathers and the Church historians have stated Gnosticism to be. So let us run "parallels," and taking the Statement sentence by sentence set it side by side with the beliefs these avowed heretics held:

1. "There is no life, truth, intelligence, nor substance in matter."

Right off the bat we have an anti-Gnostic conviction. The Gnostics asserted (1) the reality of matter; (2) the eternity of matter; (3) the reality of evil; and (4) the eternity of evil, beliefs as totally inimical to Christian Science as they were to the early Church. Hear the Fathers: Orthodox Bishop Alexander of Lycopolis exclaimed against these heretics: "They say that God sent virtue into matter." But, "The things which are with God admit of no fellowship with matter." "They allege," wrote Orthodox Bishop Hippolytus with distaste, "that He made all things out of matter . . . They hold that Evil is a material substance, equal and opposite to good."

And Archelaus, in his Disputation with Manes, the Gnostic leader, answers thus: "There is but one only inconvertible substance, the divine substance, eternal and invisible, as is known to all."

Warns St. Gregory of Nazianzen: "Flee from the matter and darkness of Manes!"

Scoffs Tertullian: "They will have it that God made all things out of Matter . . . They give divine attributes to Matter and so make two Gods!" "Matter is nowhere!" And he proves it by the Bible: "We meet with Earth, but Matter we do not meet with. I ask then, since Matter is not mentioned in Scripture, how can the term Earth be applied to it, which marks a substance of another kind?" To deny the existence of matter is not to deny the existence of things. He was not stupid.

Jeers Bishop Methodius at the Gnostics: "You wish for the existence of matter!" So much in the slough of matter were the Gnostics that St. Augustine, who had been with them for nine years until he turned to a purer religion, stated: "They could conceive of no non-material existence." And he added: "Matter in itself can neither have being, nor be known." The Church Father opposed these heretics because, as Hans Jonas says, in his "The Gnostic Religion": "They believed matter real and an attacker."

2. "All is infinite Mind and its infinite manifestation, for God is All-in-all."

The Gnostics accepted none of this, because they were Dualists, believing "in two co-equal and co-eternal powers of Good and Evil. From all eternity these two have existed side by side: Light and Darkness, Good and Evil, God and matter. Neither can destroy the other" (Gerald Bonner).

This doctrine of Dualism denies the Omnipotence of Deity,

letting the good God merely share or divide His power with an evil god. A dogma highly offensive to the orthodox, who truly knew God to be Omnipotent. Mrs. Eddy counters this obnoxious doctrine exactly as did the Fathers:

> This admission that there can be material substance requires another admission—namely, that Spirit is not infinite and that matter is self-creative, self-existent, and eternal. From this it would follow that there are two eternal causes, warring forever with each other; and yet we say that Spirit is supreme and all presence.

Nowhere have I found this noxious Gnostic nonsense so much as mentioned in Walter Martin's "Cult" books. Instead, he has stated that some Gnostic writings "reflect the idea that the material universe is not to be considered as reality and that the only true reality is spirit or mind."

Where? Apparently the Church Fathers did not know this, for they went on blithely attacking this false belief in the reality of matter and evil! I should like to see this needle in a haystack—a Gnosticism which denied reality to matter! If Reverend Martin is right, the information in Volume One of Early Church Fathers is wrong, for it states: "All Gnostic systems depend upon a principle that is at variance with Christianity—the dualism of matter and spirit."

"All is infinite Mind" contradicts Gnosticism. Says Bishop Alexander: "They lay down two principles, God and matter. And yet God does not stand in need of matter to make anything, since in His Mind all things substantially exist." Go to the head of the class, Bishop Alexander, along with Tertullian. You, too, St. John of Damascus, for affirming in your Exposition of the Orthodox Faith: "It is by thought that He creates, and that is the basis of His work." None of you fell for that "Matter" baloney.

3. "Spirit is immortal Truth; matter is mortal error."

A Gnostic would reject this statement, for he affirms that matter is a superior partner in the firm of Matter and Mind, and is real—not "unreal"—and immortal—not "temporal." Like other antignostics, Rufinus complains, "They assert the existence of two mutually antagonistic orders of reality, one good and the other evil." It is no surprise that George Bishop, in his history of "Faith Healing" calls the Gnostic's delusion "a duality that does not exist in Christian Science."

4. "Spirit is the real and eternal; matter is the unreal and temporal."

According to Bonner, the Gnostics were such out-and-out materialists that even Spirit was to them simply a tenuous matter. An "unreal and temporal" matter was totally contrary to their dogma. "Apologists like Clement, Theophilus, and Tertullian recognized that the co-eternity of God and matter was inconsistent with the sovereignty and freedom of God." (Jaroslav Pelikan, in The Christian Tradition).

5. "Spirit is God, and man is His image and likeness. Therefore man is not material; he is spiritual."

An anti-Gnostic conclusion. Man is spiritual. But the heretics, according to the Britannica (15th edition) and in many other articles on Gnosticism, asserted that "man is material." Reverend Martin reports the same thing of them in The New Cults, p. 352, but forgets this fact when attacking the Scientific Statement of Being.

Nor do the Gnostics "deny sin." According to Irenaeus they "attempted to show that God was the author of sin." they affirmed the whole gamut of evil, its reality and eternality, including sin.

And of course it is plain that they were not "positive thinkers."

Accepting as they did Matter and Evil as eternal verities they were perforce fatalistic pessimists. Exhibits follow:

1. "Gnosticism . . . seems to be the metaphysics of despair." (Sorbonne Church historian Guitton)
2. "The predominant Gnostic sense of the evil of human existence." (Professor Wilson)
3. "It was a religion of pessimism." (Bonner)
4. "Good and evil were inextricably intermingled, with evil predominating." (Guitton)
5. "With them evil is a terrible reality." (J.F. Bethune-Baker,D.D.)

6. "The world is bad; it is under the control of evil."
   (Joseph B. Tyson, A Study of Early Christianity)

One need not have to know much about Christian Science to be aware that the Gnostics' basic beliefs were at total variance with it. However, let us close with a cheerful blast at the Gnostics of yesterday and today. In Christian Healing Mrs. Eddy writes:

"There is but one side to good,—it has no evil side: There is but one side to reality, and that is the good side.

"God is all, and in all: That finishes the question of a good and a bad side to existence. Truth is the real: Error is the unreal."

Stewart Robb
From the Anaheim Bulletin

APPENDIX II

Magna Instauratio

The soon-coming Great Restoration is prophesied in the ancient Ode of Solomon, the son of David. The Restoration will be preceded by a book:

"And His thought was like a letter; His will descended from on high, and it was sent like an arrow which is violently shot from the bow: "And many hands rushed to the letter to seize it and to take and read it: "And it escaped their fingers and they were affrighted at it and at the seal that was upon it." "Because it was not permitted to them to loose its seal: for the power that was over the seal was greater than they.

"But those who saw it went after the letter that they might know where it would alight, and who should read it and who should hear it.

"But a wheel received it and came over it:

"And there was with it a sign of the Kingdom and of the Government:

"And everything which tried to move the wheel it mowed and cut down:

"And it gathered the multitude of adversaries, and bridged the rivers and crossed over and rooted up many forests and made a broad path.

"The head went down to the feet, for down to the feet ran the wheel, and that which was a sign upon it.

"The letter was one of command, for there were included in it all regions;

"And there was seen at its head, the head which was revealed, even the Son of Truth from the Most High Father.

And he inherited and took possession of everything . And the thought of many was brought to nought. "And all the apostates hasted and fled away. And those who persecuted and were enraged became extinct.

"And the letter became a great volume, which was wholly written by the finger of God:

"And the name of the Father was on it, and of the Son and of the Holy Spirit, to rule for ever and ever. Hallelujah."

Another Restoration Prophecy

Another of the many latter-day prophecies is from the pen of Moses Maimonides (1135-1204). "Those saintly beings the prophets will carry us beyond the fleeting present and show what the future holds. We will acquire that knowledge with facility. For, from our midst will issue forth divinely illumined minds. We will not be compelled to travel far for instructions. "The promised prophet cannot alter the Law, or introduce new theories. He will only refer to, and he will disclose if needed, what Gentiles imagine their fortune tellers can unfold. "There will arise a man of the direct descent of David, who will gather our outcasts, roll away our shame, and put an end to our exile. He will make the law of truth triumphant. He will cause those to perish who oppose it. Yes, such is the drift of what we read in the Pentateuch: 'I see it but not now, I behold it but not near, a star shall shoot out of Jacob, and a sceptre rise out of Israel.'

"Israel shall acquire power. And shortly before that advent there will be a time of great distress to our people. Then the Lord will make the deliverer reveal himself and fulfill the promises made.

"As to the period at which the expected occurrence will happen, we may infer from the words of Daniel, of Isaiah and other prophets and Sages, that it will be, when Christianity and Mohammedanism grow exceedingly powerful and spread their dominions, as at present, into distant countries.

"The sign of the coming of the Messiah is the appearance of a foolish individual, daubed with the title of prophet.... The rider on an ass is the symbol of the Messiah.

"The successful influence assigned to him surpasses even that ascribed to the son of Amram (Moses). He must be wise, in forecasting consequences.

"He will not commend himself to our veneration by reason of his notable extraction, but the marvelous deeds he shall perform will show him to be the anticipated Messiah. His exact descent will not be known, till his successful career will direct people's attention to it. "After having revealed himself in the Holy Land, having gathered the dispersed of Jerusalem, received recognition from countries nearer to Palestine, the fame of our nation through him will spread Eastward and Westward, reaching at length those of South Arabia, and those still further in India, who will acknowledge the mission of our leader.

"A noteworthy circumstance will be that crowned heads will stand amazed, and feel at a loss how to oppose the overpowering influence exercised by the man, whose lofty mission they cannot deny, for its genuineness is to be self-evident.

"Still the complete ceasing of political agitation, and of bloody wars, will not happen immediately on his appearing, but after the contest with Gog and Magog."

THE END